C-1152   CAREER EXAMINATION SERIES

This is your
PASSBOOK for...

Building Repairman

Test Preparation Study Guide
Questions & Answers

COPYRIGHT NOTICE

This book is SOLELY intended for, is sold ONLY to, and its use is RESTRICTED to individual, bona fide applicants or candidates who qualify by virtue of having seriously filed applications for appropriate license, certificate, professional and/or promotional advancement, higher school matriculation, scholarship, or other legitimate requirements of education and/or governmental authorities.

This book is NOT intended for use, class instruction, tutoring, training, duplication, copying, reprinting, excerption, or adaptation, etc., by:

1) Other publishers
2) Proprietors and/or Instructors of "Coaching" and/or Preparatory Courses
3) Personnel and/or Training Divisions of commercial, industrial, and governmental organizations
4) Schools, colleges, or universities and/or their departments and staffs, including teachers and other personnel
5) Testing Agencies or Bureaus
6) Study groups which seek by the purchase of a single volume to copy and/or duplicate and/or adapt this material for use by the group as a whole without having purchased individual volumes for each of the members of the group
7) Et al.

Such persons would be in violation of appropriate Federal and State statutes.

PROVISION OF LICENSING AGREEMENTS – Recognized educational, commercial, industrial, and governmental institutions and organizations, and others legitimately engaged in educational pursuits, including training, testing, and measurement activities, may address request for a licensing agreement to the copyright owners, who will determine whether, and under what conditions, including fees and charges, the materials in this book may be used them. In other words, a licensing facility exists for the legitimate use of the material in this book on other than an individual basis. However, it is asseverated and affirmed here that the material in this book CANNOT be used without the receipt of the express permission of such a licensing agreement from the Publishers. Inquiries re licensing should be addressed to the company, attention rights and permissions department.

All rights reserved, including the right of reproduction in whole or in part, in any form or by any means, electronic or mechanical, including photocopying, recording, or by any information storage and retrieval system, without permission in writing from the Publisher.

Copyright © 2025 by
National Learning Corporation

212 Michael Drive, Syosset, NY 11791
(516) 921-8888 • www.passbooks.com
E-mail: info@passbooks.com

PASSBOOK® SERIES

THE *PASSBOOK® SERIES* has been created to prepare applicants and candidates for the ultimate academic battlefield – the examination room.

At some time in our lives, each and every one of us may be required to take an examination – for validation, matriculation, admission, qualification, registration, certification, or licensure.

Based on the assumption that every applicant or candidate has met the basic formal educational standards, has taken the required number of courses, and read the necessary texts, the *PASSBOOK® SERIES* furnishes the one special preparation which may assure passing with confidence, instead of failing with insecurity. Examination questions – together with answers – are furnished as the basic vehicle for study so that the mysteries of the examination and its compounding difficulties may be eliminated or diminished by a sure method.

This book is meant to help you pass your examination provided that you qualify and are serious in your objective.

The entire field is reviewed through the huge store of content information which is succinctly presented through a provocative and challenging approach – the question-and-answer method.

A climate of success is established by furnishing the correct answers at the end of each test.

You soon learn to recognize types of questions, forms of questions, and patterns of questioning. You may even begin to anticipate expected outcomes.

You perceive that many questions are repeated or adapted so that you can gain acute insights, which may enable you to score many sure points.

You learn how to confront new questions, or types of questions, and to attack them confidently and work out the correct answers.

You note objectives and emphases, and recognize pitfalls and dangers, so that you may make positive educational adjustments.

Moreover, you are kept fully informed in relation to new concepts, methods, practices, and directions in the field.

You discover that you are actually taking the examination all the time: you are preparing for the examination by "taking" an examination, not by reading extraneous and/or supererogatory textbooks.

In short, this PASSBOOK®, used directedly, should be an important factor in helping you to pass your test.

BUILDING REPAIRMAN

DUTIES AND RESPONSIBILITIES

Under direct supervision, assists in the routine maintenance operation and repair of buildings and structures and equipment therein operated and maintained by the agencies and authorities; performs related work.

EXAMPLES OF TYPICAL TASKS

Maintains, adjusts and makes minor repairs to building hardware and equipment. Replaces broken window and door glass. Repairs windows and sash. Makes minor repairs to masonry, woodwork, flooring and walls. Makes minor repairs to building electrical, plumbing and heating systems. Assists in relocating building equipment as directed. Keeps job and other records.

TESTS

The written test will be of the multiple-choice type and may include questions on elementary knowledge of building maintenance and repair practices including electrical, plumbing and heating systems; use of materials in maintenance and repair work; use and care of tools and equipment; simple arithmetic and record keeping; safety; dealing with the public and other employees; and other related areas.

HOW TO TAKE A TEST

I. YOU MUST PASS AN EXAMINATION

A. *WHAT EVERY CANDIDATE SHOULD KNOW*

Examination applicants often ask us for help in preparing for the written test. What can I study in advance? What kinds of questions will be asked? How will the test be given? How will the papers be graded?

As an applicant for a civil service examination, you may be wondering about some of these things. Our purpose here is to suggest effective methods of advance study and to describe civil service examinations.

Your chances for success on this examination can be increased if you know how to prepare. Those "pre-examination jitters" can be reduced if you know what to expect. You can even experience an adventure in good citizenship if you know why civil service exams are given.

B. *WHY ARE CIVIL SERVICE EXAMINATIONS GIVEN?*

Civil service examinations are important to you in two ways. As a citizen, you want public jobs filled by employees who know how to do their work. As a job seeker, you want a fair chance to compete for that job on an equal footing with other candidates. The best-known means of accomplishing this two-fold goal is the competitive examination.

Exams are widely publicized throughout the nation. They may be administered for jobs in federal, state, city, municipal, town or village governments or agencies.

Any citizen may apply, with some limitations, such as the age or residence of applicants. Your experience and education may be reviewed to see whether you meet the requirements for the particular examination. When these requirements exist, they are reasonable and applied consistently to all applicants. Thus, a competitive examination may cause you some uneasiness now, but it is your privilege and safeguard.

C. *HOW ARE CIVIL SERVICE EXAMS DEVELOPED?*

Examinations are carefully written by trained technicians who are specialists in the field known as "psychological measurement," in consultation with recognized authorities in the field of work that the test will cover. These experts recommend the subject matter areas or skills to be tested; only those knowledges or skills important to your success on the job are included. The most reliable books and source materials available are used as references. Together, the experts and technicians judge the difficulty level of the questions.

Test technicians know how to phrase questions so that the problem is clearly stated. Their ethics do not permit "trick" or "catch" questions. Questions may have been tried out on sample groups, or subjected to statistical analysis, to determine their usefulness.

Written tests are often used in combination with performance tests, ratings of training and experience, and oral interviews. All of these measures combine to form the best-known means of finding the right person for the right job.

II. HOW TO PASS THE WRITTEN TEST

A. NATURE OF THE EXAMINATION

To prepare intelligently for civil service examinations, you should know how they differ from school examinations you have taken. In school you were assigned certain definite pages to read or subjects to cover. The examination questions were quite detailed and usually emphasized memory. Civil service exams, on the other hand, try to discover your present ability to perform the duties of a position, plus your potentiality to learn these duties. In other words, a civil service exam attempts to predict how successful you will be. Questions cover such a broad area that they cannot be as minute and detailed as school exam questions.

In the public service similar kinds of work, or positions, are grouped together in one "class." This process is known as *position-classification*. All the positions in a class are paid according to the salary range for that class. One class title covers all of these positions, and they are all tested by the same examination.

B. FOUR BASIC STEPS

1) Study the announcement

How, then, can you know what subjects to study? Our best answer is: "Learn as much as possible about the class of positions for which you've applied." The exam will test the knowledge, skills and abilities needed to do the work.

Your most valuable source of information about the position you want is the official exam announcement. This announcement lists the training and experience qualifications. Check these standards and apply only if you come reasonably close to meeting them.

The brief description of the position in the examination announcement offers some clues to the subjects which will be tested. Think about the job itself. Review the duties in your mind. Can you perform them, or are there some in which you are rusty? Fill in the blank spots in your preparation.

Many jurisdictions preview the written test in the exam announcement by including a section called "Knowledge and Abilities Required," "Scope of the Examination," or some similar heading. Here you will find out specifically what fields will be tested.

2) Review your own background

Once you learn in general what the position is all about, and what you need to know to do the work, ask yourself which subjects you already know fairly well and which need improvement. You may wonder whether to concentrate on improving your strong areas or on building some background in your fields of weakness. When the announcement has specified "some knowledge" or "considerable knowledge," or has used adjectives like "beginning principles of…" or "advanced … methods," you can get a clue as to the number and difficulty of questions to be asked in any given field. More questions, and hence broader coverage, would be included for those subjects which are more important in the work. Now weigh your strengths and weaknesses against the job requirements and prepare accordingly.

3) Determine the level of the position

Another way to tell how intensively you should prepare is to understand the level of the job for which you are applying. Is it the entering level? In other words, is this the position in which beginners in a field of work are hired? Or is it an intermediate or advanced level? Sometimes this is indicated by such words as "Junior" or "Senior" in the class title. Other jurisdictions use Roman numerals to designate the level – Clerk I, Clerk II, for example. The word "Supervisor" sometimes appears in the title. If the level is not indicated by the title, check the description of duties. Will you be working under very close supervision, or will you have responsibility for independent decisions in this work?

4) Choose appropriate study materials

Now that you know the subjects to be examined and the relative amount of each subject to be covered, you can choose suitable study materials. For beginning level jobs, or even advanced ones, if you have a pronounced weakness in some aspect of your training, read a modern, standard textbook in that field. Be sure it is up to date and has general coverage. Such books are normally available at your library, and the librarian will be glad to help you locate one. For entry-level positions, questions of appropriate difficulty are chosen – neither highly advanced questions, nor those too simple. Such questions require careful thought but not advanced training.

If the position for which you are applying is technical or advanced, you will read more advanced, specialized material. If you are already familiar with the basic principles of your field, elementary textbooks would waste your time. Concentrate on advanced textbooks and technical periodicals. Think through the concepts and review difficult problems in your field.

These are all general sources. You can get more ideas on your own initiative, following these leads. For example, training manuals and publications of the government agency which employs workers in your field can be useful, particularly for technical and professional positions. A letter or visit to the government department involved may result in more specific study suggestions, and certainly will provide you with a more definite idea of the exact nature of the position you are seeking.

III. KINDS OF TESTS

Tests are used for purposes other than measuring knowledge and ability to perform specified duties. For some positions, it is equally important to test ability to make adjustments to new situations or to profit from training. In others, basic mental abilities not dependent on information are essential. Questions which test these things may not appear as pertinent to the duties of the position as those which test for knowledge and information. Yet they are often highly important parts of a fair examination. For very general questions, it is almost impossible to help you direct your study efforts. What we can do is to point out some of the more common of these general abilities needed in public service positions and describe some typical questions.

1) General information

Broad, general information has been found useful for predicting job success in some kinds of work. This is tested in a variety of ways, from vocabulary lists to questions about current events. Basic background in some field of work, such as sociology or economics, may be sampled in a group of questions. Often these are principles which have become familiar to most persons through exposure rather than through formal training. It is difficult to advise you how to study for these questions; being alert to the world around you is our best suggestion.

2) Verbal ability

An example of an ability needed in many positions is verbal or language ability. Verbal ability is, in brief, the ability to use and understand words. Vocabulary and grammar tests are typical measures of this ability. Reading comprehension or paragraph interpretation questions are common in many kinds of civil service tests. You are given a paragraph of written material and asked to find its central meaning.

3) Numerical ability

Number skills can be tested by the familiar arithmetic problem, by checking paired lists of numbers to see which are alike and which are different, or by interpreting charts and graphs. In the latter test, a graph may be printed in the test booklet which you are asked to use as the basis for answering questions.

4) Observation

A popular test for law-enforcement positions is the observation test. A picture is shown to you for several minutes, then taken away. Questions about the picture test your ability to observe both details and larger elements.

5) Following directions

In many positions in the public service, the employee must be able to carry out written instructions dependably and accurately. You may be given a chart with several columns, each column listing a variety of information. The questions require you to carry out directions involving the information given in the chart.

6) Skills and aptitudes

Performance tests effectively measure some manual skills and aptitudes. When the skill is one in which you are trained, such as typing or shorthand, you can practice. These tests are often very much like those given in business school or high school courses. For many of the other skills and aptitudes, however, no short-time preparation can be made. Skills and abilities natural to you or that you have developed throughout your lifetime are being tested.

Many of the general questions just described provide all the data needed to answer the questions and ask you to use your reasoning ability to find the answers. Your best preparation for these tests, as well as for tests of facts and ideas, is to be at your physical and mental best. You, no doubt, have your own methods of getting into an exam-taking mood and keeping "in shape." The next section lists some ideas on this subject.

IV. KINDS OF QUESTIONS

Only rarely is the "essay" question, which you answer in narrative form, used in civil service tests. Civil service tests are usually of the short-answer type. Full instructions for answering these questions will be given to you at the examination. But in case this is your first experience with short-answer questions and separate answer sheets, here is what you need to know:

1) Multiple-choice Questions

Most popular of the short-answer questions is the "multiple choice" or "best answer" question. It can be used, for example, to test for factual knowledge, ability to solve problems or judgment in meeting situations found at work.

A multiple-choice question is normally one of three types—
- It can begin with an incomplete statement followed by several possible endings. You are to find the one ending which *best* completes the statement, although some of the others may not be entirely wrong.
- It can also be a complete statement in the form of a question which is answered by choosing one of the statements listed.

- It can be in the form of a problem – again you select the best answer.

Here is an example of a multiple-choice question with a discussion which should give you some clues as to the method for choosing the right answer:

When an employee has a complaint about his assignment, the action which will *best* help him overcome his difficulty is to
- A. discuss his difficulty with his coworkers
- B. take the problem to the head of the organization
- C. take the problem to the person who gave him the assignment
- D. say nothing to anyone about his complaint

In answering this question, you should study each of the choices to find which is best. Consider choice "A" – Certainly an employee may discuss his complaint with fellow employees, but no change or improvement can result, and the complaint remains unresolved. Choice "B" is a poor choice since the head of the organization probably does not know what assignment you have been given, and taking your problem to him is known as "going over the head" of the supervisor. The supervisor, or person who made the assignment, is the person who can clarify it or correct any injustice. Choice "C" is, therefore, correct. To say nothing, as in choice "D," is unwise. Supervisors have and interest in knowing the problems employees are facing, and the employee is seeking a solution to his problem.

2) True/False Questions

The "true/false" or "right/wrong" form of question is sometimes used. Here a complete statement is given. Your job is to decide whether the statement is right or wrong.

SAMPLE: A roaming cell-phone call to a nearby city costs less than a non-roaming call to a distant city.

This statement is wrong, or false, since roaming calls are more expensive.

This is not a complete list of all possible question forms, although most of the others are variations of these common types. You will always get complete directions for answering questions. Be sure you understand *how* to mark your answers – ask questions until you do.

V. RECORDING YOUR ANSWERS

Computer terminals are used more and more today for many different kinds of exams.

For an examination with very few applicants, you may be told to record your answers in the test booklet itself. Separate answer sheets are much more common. If this separate answer sheet is to be scored by machine – and this is often the case – it is highly important that you mark your answers correctly in order to get credit.

An electronic scoring machine is often used in civil service offices because of the speed with which papers can be scored. Machine-scored answer sheets must be marked with a pencil, which will be given to you. This pencil has a high graphite content which responds to the electronic scoring machine. As a matter of fact, stray dots may register as answers, so do not let your pencil rest on the answer sheet while you are pondering the correct answer. Also, if your pencil lead breaks or is otherwise defective, ask for another.

Since the answer sheet will be dropped in a slot in the scoring machine, be careful not to bend the corners or get the paper crumpled.

The answer sheet normally has five vertical columns of numbers, with 30 numbers to a column. These numbers correspond to the question numbers in your test booklet. After each number, going across the page are four or five pairs of dotted lines. These short dotted lines have small letters or numbers above them. The first two pairs may also have a "T" or "F" above the letters. This indicates that the first two pairs only are to be used if the questions are of the true-false type. If the questions are multiple choice, disregard the "T" and "F" and pay attention only to the small letters or numbers.

Answer your questions in the manner of the sample that follows:

32. The largest city in the United States is
    A. Washington, D.C.
    B. New York City
    C. Chicago
    D. Detroit
    E. San Francisco

1) Choose the answer you think is best. (New York City is the largest, so "B" is correct.)
2) Find the row of dotted lines numbered the same as the question you are answering. (Find row number 32)
3) Find the pair of dotted lines corresponding to the answer. (Find the pair of lines under the mark "B.")
4) Make a solid black mark between the dotted lines.

VI. BEFORE THE TEST

Common sense will help you find procedures to follow to get ready for an examination. Too many of us, however, overlook these sensible measures. Indeed, nervousness and fatigue have been found to be the most serious reasons why applicants fail to do their best on civil service tests. Here is a list of reminders:

- Begin your preparation early – Don't wait until the last minute to go scurrying around for books and materials or to find out what the position is all about.
- Prepare continuously – An hour a night for a week is better than an all-night cram session. This has been definitely established. What is more, a night a week for a month will return better dividends than crowding your study into a shorter period of time.
- Locate the place of the exam – You have been sent a notice telling you when and where to report for the examination. If the location is in a different town or otherwise unfamiliar to you, it would be well to inquire the best route and learn something about the building.
- Relax the night before the test – Allow your mind to rest. Do not study at all that night. Plan some mild recreation or diversion; then go to bed early and get a good night's sleep.
- Get up early enough to make a leisurely trip to the place for the test – This way unforeseen events, traffic snarls, unfamiliar buildings, etc. will not upset you.
- Dress comfortably – A written test is not a fashion show. You will be known by number and not by name, so wear something comfortable.

- Leave excess paraphernalia at home – Shopping bags and odd bundles will get in your way. You need bring only the items mentioned in the official notice you received; usually everything you need is provided. Do not bring reference books to the exam. They will only confuse those last minutes and be taken away from you when in the test room.
- Arrive somewhat ahead of time – If because of transportation schedules you must get there very early, bring a newspaper or magazine to take your mind off yourself while waiting.
- Locate the examination room – When you have found the proper room, you will be directed to the seat or part of the room where you will sit. Sometimes you are given a sheet of instructions to read while you are waiting. Do not fill out any forms until you are told to do so; just read them and be prepared.
- Relax and prepare to listen to the instructions
- If you have any physical problem that may keep you from doing your best, be sure to tell the test administrator. If you are sick or in poor health, you really cannot do your best on the exam. You can come back and take the test some other time.

VII. AT THE TEST

The day of the test is here and you have the test booklet in your hand. The temptation to get going is very strong. Caution! There is more to success than knowing the right answers. You must know how to identify your papers and understand variations in the type of short-answer question used in this particular examination. Follow these suggestions for maximum results from your efforts:

1) Cooperate with the monitor

The test administrator has a duty to create a situation in which you can be as much at ease as possible. He will give instructions, tell you when to begin, check to see that you are marking your answer sheet correctly, and so on. He is not there to guard you, although he will see that your competitors do not take unfair advantage. He wants to help you do your best.

2) Listen to all instructions

Don't jump the gun! Wait until you understand all directions. In most civil service tests you get more time than you need to answer the questions. So don't be in a hurry. Read each word of instructions until you clearly understand the meaning. Study the examples, listen to all announcements and follow directions. Ask questions if you do not understand what to do.

3) Identify your papers

Civil service exams are usually identified by number only. You will be assigned a number; you must not put your name on your test papers. Be sure to copy your number correctly. Since more than one exam may be given, copy your exact examination title.

4) Plan your time

Unless you are told that a test is a "speed" or "rate of work" test, speed itself is usually not important. Time enough to answer all the questions will be provided, but this does not mean that you have all day. An overall time limit has been set. Divide the total time (in minutes) by the number of questions to determine the approximate time you have for each question.

5) Do not linger over difficult questions

If you come across a difficult question, mark it with a paper clip (useful to have along) and come back to it when you have been through the booklet. One caution if you do this – be sure to skip a number on your answer sheet as well. Check often to be sure that you have not lost your place and that you are marking in the row numbered the same as the question you are answering.

6) Read the questions

Be sure you know what the question asks! Many capable people are unsuccessful because they failed to *read* the questions correctly.

7) Answer all questions

Unless you have been instructed that a penalty will be deducted for incorrect answers, it is better to guess than to omit a question.

8) Speed tests

It is often better NOT to guess on speed tests. It has been found that on timed tests people are tempted to spend the last few seconds before time is called in marking answers at random – without even reading them – in the hope of picking up a few extra points. To discourage this practice, the instructions may warn you that your score will be "corrected" for guessing. That is, a penalty will be applied. The incorrect answers will be deducted from the correct ones, or some other penalty formula will be used.

9) Review your answers

If you finish before time is called, go back to the questions you guessed or omitted to give them further thought. Review other answers if you have time.

10) Return your test materials

If you are ready to leave before others have finished or time is called, take ALL your materials to the monitor and leave quietly. Never take any test material with you. The monitor can discover whose papers are not complete, and taking a test booklet may be grounds for disqualification.

VIII. EXAMINATION TECHNIQUES

1) Read the general instructions carefully. These are usually printed on the first page of the exam booklet. As a rule, these instructions refer to the timing of the examination; the fact that you should not start work until the signal and must stop work at a signal, etc. If there are any *special* instructions, such as a choice of questions to be answered, make sure that you note this instruction carefully.

2) When you are ready to start work on the examination, that is as soon as the signal has been given, read the instructions to each question booklet, underline any key words or phrases, such as *least, best, outline, describe* and the like. In this way you will tend to answer as requested rather than discover on reviewing your paper that you *listed without describing*, that you selected the *worst* choice rather than the *best* choice, etc.

3) If the examination is of the objective or multiple-choice type – that is, each question will also give a series of possible answers: A, B, C or D, and you are called upon to select the best answer and write the letter next to that answer on your answer paper – it is advisable to start answering each question in turn. There may be anywhere from 50 to 100 such questions in the three or four hours allotted and you can see how much time would be taken if you read through all the questions before beginning to answer any. Furthermore, if you come across a question or group of questions which you know would be difficult to answer, it would undoubtedly affect your handling of all the other questions.

4) If the examination is of the essay type and contains but a few questions, it is a moot point as to whether you should read all the questions before starting to answer any one. Of course, if you are given a choice – say five out of seven and the like – then it is essential to read all the questions so you can eliminate the two that are most difficult. If, however, you are asked to answer all the questions, there may be danger in trying to answer the easiest one first because you may find that you will spend too much time on it. The best technique is to answer the first question, then proceed to the second, etc.

5) Time your answers. Before the exam begins, write down the time it started, then add the time allowed for the examination and write down the time it must be completed, then divide the time available somewhat as follows:
   - If 3-1/2 hours are allowed, that would be 210 minutes. If you have 80 objective-type questions, that would be an average of 2-1/2 minutes per question. Allow yourself no more than 2 minutes per question, or a total of 160 minutes, which will permit about 50 minutes to review.
   - If for the time allotment of 210 minutes there are 7 essay questions to answer, that would average about 30 minutes a question. Give yourself only 25 minutes per question so that you have about 35 minutes to review.

6) The most important instruction is to *read each question* and make sure you know what is wanted. The second most important instruction is to *time yourself properly* so that you answer every question. The third most important instruction is to *answer every question*. Guess if you have to but include something for each question. Remember that you will receive no credit for a blank and will probably receive some credit if you write something in answer to an essay question. If you guess a letter – say "B" for a multiple-choice question – you may have guessed right. If you leave a blank as an answer to a multiple-choice question, the examiners may respect your feelings but it will not add a point to your score. Some exams may penalize you for wrong answers, so in such cases *only*, you may not want to guess unless you have some basis for your answer.

7) Suggestions
   a. Objective-type questions
      1. Examine the question booklet for proper sequence of pages and questions
      2. Read all instructions carefully
      3. Skip any question which seems too difficult; return to it after all other questions have been answered
      4. Apportion your time properly; do not spend too much time on any single question or group of questions

5. Note and underline key words – *all, most, fewest, least, best, worst, same, opposite,* etc.
6. Pay particular attention to negatives
7. Note unusual option, e.g., unduly long, short, complex, different or similar in content to the body of the question
8. Observe the use of "hedging" words – *probably, may, most likely,* etc.
9. Make sure that your answer is put next to the same number as the question
10. Do not second-guess unless you have good reason to believe the second answer is definitely more correct
11. Cross out original answer if you decide another answer is more accurate; do not erase until you are ready to hand your paper in
12. Answer all questions; guess unless instructed otherwise
13. Leave time for review

   b. Essay questions
     1. Read each question carefully
     2. Determine exactly what is wanted. Underline key words or phrases.
     3. Decide on outline or paragraph answer
     4. Include many different points and elements unless asked to develop any one or two points or elements
     5. Show impartiality by giving pros and cons unless directed to select one side only
     6. Make and write down any assumptions you find necessary to answer the questions
     7. Watch your English, grammar, punctuation and choice of words
     8. Time your answers; don't crowd material

8) Answering the essay question

Most essay questions can be answered by framing the specific response around several key words or ideas. Here are a few such key words or ideas:

M's: manpower, materials, methods, money, management
P's: purpose, program, policy, plan, procedure, practice, problems, pitfalls, personnel, public relations

   a. Six basic steps in handling problems:
     1. Preliminary plan and background development
     2. Collect information, data and facts
     3. Analyze and interpret information, data and facts
     4. Analyze and develop solutions as well as make recommendations
     5. Prepare report and sell recommendations
     6. Install recommendations and follow up effectiveness

   b. Pitfalls to avoid
     1. *Taking things for granted* – A statement of the situation does not necessarily imply that each of the elements is necessarily true; for example, a complaint may be invalid and biased so that all that can be taken for granted is that a complaint has been registered

2. *Considering only one side of a situation* – Wherever possible, indicate several alternatives and then point out the reasons you selected the best one
3. *Failing to indicate follow up* – Whenever your answer indicates action on your part, make certain that you will take proper follow-up action to see how successful your recommendations, procedures or actions turn out to be
4. *Taking too long in answering any single question* – Remember to time your answers properly

IX. AFTER THE TEST

Scoring procedures differ in detail among civil service jurisdictions although the general principles are the same. Whether the papers are hand-scored or graded by machine we have described, they are nearly always graded by number. That is, the person who marks the paper knows only the number – never the name – of the applicant. Not until all the papers have been graded will they be matched with names. If other tests, such as training and experience or oral interview ratings have been given, scores will be combined. Different parts of the examination usually have different weights. For example, the written test might count 60 percent of the final grade, and a rating of training and experience 40 percent. In many jurisdictions, veterans will have a certain number of points added to their grades.

After the final grade has been determined, the names are placed in grade order and an eligible list is established. There are various methods for resolving ties between those who get the same final grade – probably the most common is to place first the name of the person whose application was received first. Job offers are made from the eligible list in the order the names appear on it. You will be notified of your grade and your rank as soon as all these computations have been made. This will be done as rapidly as possible.

People who are found to meet the requirements in the announcement are called "eligibles." Their names are put on a list of eligible candidates. An eligible's chances of getting a job depend on how high he stands on this list and how fast agencies are filling jobs from the list.

When a job is to be filled from a list of eligibles, the agency asks for the names of people on the list of eligibles for that job. When the civil service commission receives this request, it sends to the agency the names of the three people highest on this list. Or, if the job to be filled has specialized requirements, the office sends the agency the names of the top three persons who meet these requirements from the general list.

The appointing officer makes a choice from among the three people whose names were sent to him. If the selected person accepts the appointment, the names of the others are put back on the list to be considered for future openings.

That is the rule in hiring from all kinds of eligible lists, whether they are for typist, carpenter, chemist, or something else. For every vacancy, the appointing officer has his choice of any one of the top three eligibles on the list. This explains why the person whose name is on top of the list sometimes does not get an appointment when some of the persons lower on the list do. If the appointing officer chooses the second or third eligible, the No. 1 eligible does not get a job at once, but stays on the list until he is appointed or the list is terminated.

X. HOW TO PASS THE INTERVIEW TEST

The examination for which you applied requires an oral interview test. You have already taken the written test and you are now being called for the interview test – the final part of the formal examination.

You may think that it is not possible to prepare for an interview test and that there are no procedures to follow during an interview. Our purpose is to point out some things you can do in advance that will help you and some good rules to follow and pitfalls to avoid while you are being interviewed.

What is an interview supposed to test?

The written examination is designed to test the technical knowledge and competence of the candidate; the oral is designed to evaluate intangible qualities, not readily measured otherwise, and to establish a list showing the relative fitness of each candidate – as measured against his competitors – for the position sought. Scoring is not on the basis of "right" and "wrong," but on a sliding scale of values ranging from "not passable" to "outstanding." As a matter of fact, it is possible to achieve a relatively low score without a single "incorrect" answer because of evident weakness in the qualities being measured.

Occasionally, an examination may consist entirely of an oral test – either an individual or a group oral. In such cases, information is sought concerning the technical knowledges and abilities of the candidate, since there has been no written examination for this purpose. More commonly, however, an oral test is used to supplement a written examination.

Who conducts interviews?

The composition of oral boards varies among different jurisdictions. In nearly all, a representative of the personnel department serves as chairman. One of the members of the board may be a representative of the department in which the candidate would work. In some cases, "outside experts" are used, and, frequently, a businessman or some other representative of the general public is asked to serve. Labor and management or other special groups may be represented. The aim is to secure the services of experts in the appropriate field.

However the board is composed, it is a good idea (and not at all improper or unethical) to ascertain in advance of the interview who the members are and what groups they represent. When you are introduced to them, you will have some idea of their backgrounds and interests, and at least you will not stutter and stammer over their names.

What should be done before the interview?

While knowledge about the board members is useful and takes some of the surprise element out of the interview, there is other preparation which is more substantive. It *is* possible to prepare for an oral interview – in several ways:

1) Keep a copy of your application and review it carefully before the interview

This may be the only document before the oral board, and the starting point of the interview. Know what education and experience you have listed there, and the sequence and dates of all of it. Sometimes the board will ask you to review the highlights of your experience for them; you should not have to hem and haw doing it.

2) Study the class specification and the examination announcement

Usually, the oral board has one or both of these to guide them. The qualities, characteristics or knowledges required by the position sought are stated in these documents. They offer valuable clues as to the nature of the oral interview. For example, if the job involves supervisory responsibilities, the announcement will usually indicate that knowledge of modern supervisory methods and the qualifications of the candidate as a supervisor will be tested. If so, you can expect such questions, frequently in the form of a hypothetical situation which you are expected to solve. NEVER go into an oral without knowledge of the duties and responsibilities of the job you seek.

3) Think through each qualification required

Try to visualize the kind of questions you would ask if you were a board member. How well could you answer them? Try especially to appraise your own knowledge and background in each area, *measured against the job sought*, and identify any areas in which you are weak. Be critical and realistic – do not flatter yourself.

4) Do some general reading in areas in which you feel you may be weak

For example, if the job involves supervision and your past experience has NOT, some general reading in supervisory methods and practices, particularly in the field of human relations, might be useful. Do NOT study agency procedures or detailed manuals. The oral board will be testing your understanding and capacity, not your memory.

5) Get a good night's sleep and watch your general health and mental attitude

You will want a clear head at the interview. Take care of a cold or any other minor ailment, and of course, no hangovers.

What should be done on the day of the interview?

Now comes the day of the interview itself. Give yourself plenty of time to get there. Plan to arrive somewhat ahead of the scheduled time, particularly if your appointment is in the fore part of the day. If a previous candidate fails to appear, the board might be ready for you a bit early. By early afternoon an oral board is almost invariably behind schedule if there are many candidates, and you may have to wait. Take along a book or magazine to read, or your application to review, but leave any extraneous material in the waiting room when you go in for your interview. In any event, relax and compose yourself.

The matter of dress is important. The board is forming impressions about you – from your experience, your manners, your attitude, and your appearance. Give your personal appearance careful attention. Dress your best, but not your flashiest. Choose conservative, appropriate clothing, and be sure it is immaculate. This is a business interview, and your appearance should indicate that you regard it as such. Besides, being well groomed and properly dressed will help boost your confidence.

Sooner or later, someone will call your name and escort you into the interview room. *This is it.* From here on you are on your own. It is too late for any more preparation. But remember, you asked for this opportunity to prove your fitness, and you are here because your request was granted.

What happens when you go in?

The usual sequence of events will be as follows: The clerk (who is often the board stenographer) will introduce you to the chairman of the oral board, who will introduce you to the other members of the board. Acknowledge the introductions before you sit down. Do not be surprised if you find a microphone facing you or a stenotypist sitting by. Oral interviews are usually recorded in the event of an appeal or other review.

Usually the chairman of the board will open the interview by reviewing the highlights of your education and work experience from your application – primarily for the benefit of the other members of the board, as well as to get the material into the record. Do not interrupt or comment unless there is an error or significant misinterpretation; if that is the case, do not hesitate. But do not quibble about insignificant matters. Also, he will usually ask you some question about your education, experience or your present job – partly to get you to start talking and to establish the interviewing "rapport." He may start the actual questioning, or turn it over to one of the other members. Frequently, each member undertakes the questioning on a particular area, one in which he is perhaps most competent, so you can expect each member to participate in the examination. Because time is limited, you may also expect some rather abrupt switches in the direction the questioning takes, so do not be upset by it. Normally, a board member will not pursue a single line of questioning unless he discovers a particular strength or weakness.

After each member has participated, the chairman will usually ask whether any member has any further questions, then will ask you if you have anything you wish to add. Unless you are expecting this question, it may floor you. Worse, it may start you off on an extended, extemporaneous speech. The board is not usually seeking more information. The question is principally to offer you a last opportunity to present further qualifications or to indicate that you have nothing to add. So, if you feel that a significant qualification or characteristic has been overlooked, it is proper to point it out in a sentence or so. Do not compliment the board on the thoroughness of their examination – they have been sketchy, and you know it. If you wish, merely say, "No thank you, I have nothing further to add." This is a point where you can "talk yourself out" of a good impression or fail to present an important bit of information. Remember, *you close the interview yourself.*

The chairman will then say, "That is all, Mr. _____, thank you." Do not be startled; the interview is over, and quicker than you think. Thank him, gather your belongings and take your leave. Save your sigh of relief for the other side of the door.

How to put your best foot forward

Throughout this entire process, you may feel that the board individually and collectively is trying to pierce your defenses, seek out your hidden weaknesses and embarrass and confuse you. Actually, this is not true. They are obliged to make an appraisal of your qualifications for the job you are seeking, and they want to see you in your best light. Remember, they must interview all candidates and a non-cooperative candidate may become a failure in spite of their best efforts to bring out his qualifications. Here are 15 suggestions that will help you:

1) Be natural – Keep your attitude confident, not cocky

If you are not confident that you can do the job, do not expect the board to be. Do not apologize for your weaknesses, try to bring out your strong points. The board is interested in a positive, not negative, presentation. Cockiness will antagonize any board member and make him wonder if you are covering up a weakness by a false show of strength.

2) Get comfortable, but don't lounge or sprawl

Sit erectly but not stiffly. A careless posture may lead the board to conclude that you are careless in other things, or at least that you are not impressed by the importance of the occasion. Either conclusion is natural, even if incorrect. Do not fuss with your clothing, a pencil or an ashtray. Your hands may occasionally be useful to emphasize a point; do not let them become a point of distraction.

3) Do not wisecrack or make small talk

This is a serious situation, and your attitude should show that you consider it as such. Further, the time of the board is limited – they do not want to waste it, and neither should you.

4) Do not exaggerate your experience or abilities

In the first place, from information in the application or other interviews and sources, the board may know more about you than you think. Secondly, you probably will not get away with it. An experienced board is rather adept at spotting such a situation, so do not take the chance.

5) If you know a board member, do not make a point of it, yet do not hide it

Certainly you are not fooling him, and probably not the other members of the board. Do not try to take advantage of your acquaintanceship – it will probably do you little good.

6) Do not dominate the interview

Let the board do that. They will give you the clues – do not assume that you have to do all the talking. Realize that the board has a number of questions to ask you, and do not try to take up all the interview time by showing off your extensive knowledge of the answer to the first one.

7) Be attentive

You only have 20 minutes or so, and you should keep your attention at its sharpest throughout. When a member is addressing a problem or question to you, give him your undivided attention. Address your reply principally to him, but do not exclude the other board members.

8) Do not interrupt

A board member may be stating a problem for you to analyze. He will ask you a question when the time comes. Let him state the problem, and wait for the question.

9) Make sure you understand the question

Do not try to answer until you are sure what the question is. If it is not clear, restate it in your own words or ask the board member to clarify it for you. However, do not haggle about minor elements.

10) Reply promptly but not hastily

A common entry on oral board rating sheets is "candidate responded readily," or "candidate hesitated in replies." Respond as promptly and quickly as you can, but do not jump to a hasty, ill-considered answer.

11) Do not be peremptory in your answers

A brief answer is proper – but do not fire your answer back. That is a losing game from your point of view. The board member can probably ask questions much faster than you can answer them.

12) Do not try to create the answer you think the board member wants

He is interested in what kind of mind you have and how it works – not in playing games. Furthermore, he can usually spot this practice and will actually grade you down on it.

13) Do not switch sides in your reply merely to agree with a board member

Frequently, a member will take a contrary position merely to draw you out and to see if you are willing and able to defend your point of view. Do not start a debate, yet do not surrender a good position. If a position is worth taking, it is worth defending.

14) Do not be afraid to admit an error in judgment if you are shown to be wrong

The board knows that you are forced to reply without any opportunity for careful consideration. Your answer may be demonstrably wrong. If so, admit it and get on with the interview.

15) Do not dwell at length on your present job

The opening question may relate to your present assignment. Answer the question but do not go into an extended discussion. You are being examined for a *new* job, not your present one. As a matter of fact, try to phrase ALL your answers in terms of the job for which you are being examined.

Basis of Rating

Probably you will forget most of these "do's" and "don'ts" when you walk into the oral interview room. Even remembering them all will not ensure you a passing grade. Perhaps you did not have the qualifications in the first place. But remembering them will help you to put your best foot forward, without treading on the toes of the board members.

Rumor and popular opinion to the contrary notwithstanding, an oral board wants you to make the best appearance possible. They know you are under pressure – but they also want to see how you respond to it as a guide to what your reaction would be under the pressures of the job you seek. They will be influenced by the degree of poise you display, the personal traits you show and the manner in which you respond.

ABOUT THIS BOOK

This book contains tests divided into Examination Sections. Go through each test, answering every question in the margin. We have also attached a sample answer sheet at the back of the book that can be removed and used. At the end of each test look at the answer key and check your answers. On the ones you got wrong, look at the right answer choice and learn. Do not fill in the answers first. Do not memorize the questions and answers, but understand the answer and principles involved. On your test, the questions will likely be different from the samples. Questions are changed and new ones added. If you understand these past questions you should have success with any changes that arise. Tests may consist of several types of questions. We have additional books on each subject should more study be advisable or necessary for you. Finally, the more you study, the better prepared you will be. This book is intended to be the last thing you study before you walk into the examination room. Prior study of relevant texts is also recommended. NLC publishes some of these in our Fundamental Series. Knowledge and good sense are important factors in passing your exam. Good luck also helps. So now study this Passbook, absorb the material contained within and take that knowledge into the examination. Then do your best to pass that exam.

EXAMINATION SECTION

EXAMINATION SECTION
TEST 1

DIRECTIONS: Each question or incomplete statement is followed by several suggested answers or completions. Select the one that BEST answers the question or completes the statement. *PRINT THE LETTER OF THE CORRECT ANSWER IN THE SPACE AT THE RIGHT.*

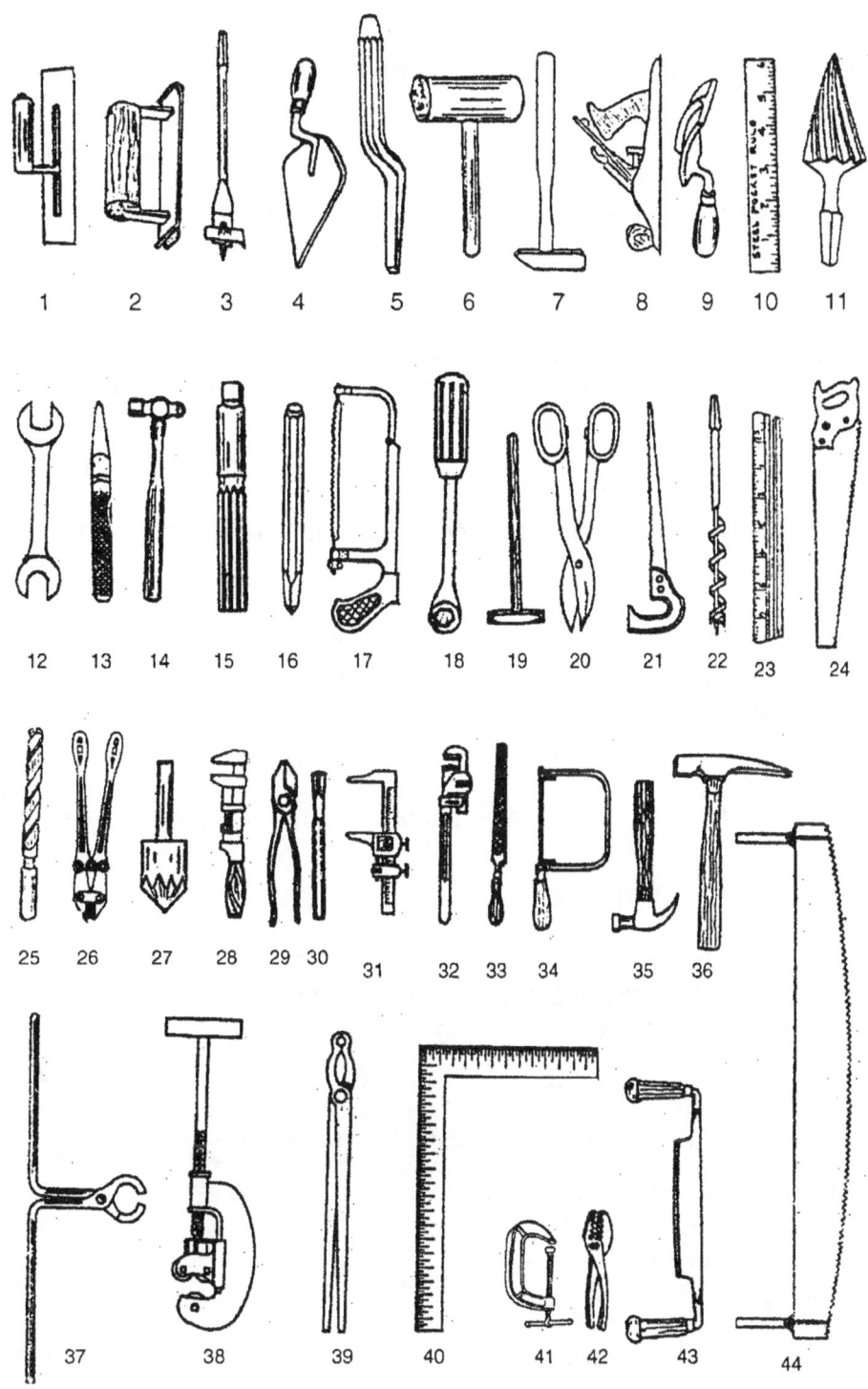

1

1. Of the following, which group of three tools is used *most nearly* in the same way?   1._____
   A. Tools 4, 21, 39   B. Tools 11, 16, 42
   C. Tools 14, 35, 36   D. Tools 5, 6, 13

2. If you want to cut a disc out of sheet metal, you should use tool no.   2._____
   A. 20   B. 26   C. 29   D. 38

3. Tool number 25 is ordinarily NOT used alone; it should be used with tool no.   3._____
   A. 28   B. 35
   C. 39   D. another tool not pictured

4. To split a brick in half you should FIRST chip the line of division all the way around the brick with tool no.   4._____
   A. 14   B. 24   C. 34   D. 36

5. To repair wide cracks in a wood floor you should glue a thin strip of wood into the crack and then level it even with the surrounding floor surface. To level this strip of wood you should use tool no.   5._____
   A. 1   B. 8   C. 24   D. 33

6. To smooth a newly laid concrete surface so that it is free of ripples and marks, you should use tool no.   6._____
   A. 1   B. 6   C. 8   D. 9

7. To measure the *outside* diameter of a section of pipe MOST accurately, the tool that should be used is tool no.   7._____
   A. 10   B. 23   C. 31   D. 40

8. The BEST tool to use to cut a curved pattern in a 1/4 inch-thick sheet of plywood is tool no.   8._____
   A. 17   B. 24   C. 34   D. 43

9. If you, as a member of a repair crew, plan to cut a rectangular piece of plywood measuring 18" x 12" out of a larger rectangular piece measuring 30" x 24", the tool that will BEST help lay out the lines and check the angles is number   9._____
   A. 10   B. 23   C. 31   D. 40

10. Either end of tool 12 can be *properly* used for the purpose of   10._____
    A. fitting into the handle of another tool
    B. turning nuts or bolts
    C. laying out angles
    D. pulling nails

11. Tools 22, 24, 35 and 40 have in common that fact that they are used *primarily* in   11._____
    A. masonry   B. plumbing
    C. sheet metal work   D. woodworking

12. Which tool requires the use of BOTH hands on the tool to operate it properly?   12.____
    A. Tool 8   B. Tool 12   C. Tool 20   D. Tool 24

13. Of the following, the tool designed to be used for turning nuts of various sizes is tool no.   13.____
    A. 19   B. 28   C. 29   D. 31

14. To cut a section of pipe to the required length, the MOST appropriate tool is number   14.____
    A. 20   B. 29   C. 31   D. 38

15. In the picture below of a roof, which one of the numbered arrows points to the "flashing"?   15.____
    A. 1   B. 2   C. 3   D. 4

16. The function of glazier's points is to   16.____
    A. keep the putty from dirtying the glass
    B. make it easy to cut glass in a straight line
    C. hold a pane of glass in place
    D. aid in applying putty evenly around the glass

17. It is *desirable* for a putty knife used for patching plaster cracks to be flexible because a flexible putty knife   17.____
    A. makes it difficult for the user to cut his hands while applying the plaster
    B. is easier to keep clean than one made of rigid material
    C. can press the patching materials into the crack, filling it completely
    D. makes it possible to pick up the exact amount of plaster required

18. Using a fuse with a *larger* rated capacity than that of the circuit is   18.____
    A. *advisable;* such use prevents the fuse from blowing
    B. *advisable;* larger capacity fuses last longer than smaller capacity fuses
    C. *inadvisable;* larger capacity fuses are more expensive than smaller capacity fuses
    D. *inadvisable;* such use may cause a fire

19. You can MOST easily tell when a screw-in type fuse has blown because the center of the strip of metal in the fuse is   19.____
    A. broken   B. visible
    C. nicked   D. cool to the touch

20. In the picture below, which of the numbered arrows points to the door "jamb"? 20._____

   A. 1   B. 2   C. 3   D. 4

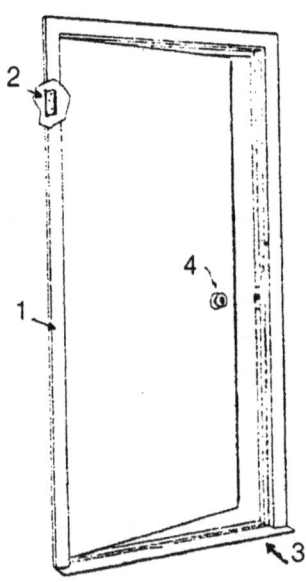

21. Of the following, the MAIN reason why flashing is used in the building trade is to make an area 21._____

   A. decorative   B. watertight   C. level   D. heat-resistant

22. To prepare a ready-mixed concrete material for use, you FIRST add 22._____

   A. gravel   B. salt   C. sand   D. water

23. When working on wet floors with an electrically powered tool, additional safety against electric shock can BEST be provided by 23._____

   A. a longer electric cord   B. an AC-DC converter
   C. rubber gloves   D. loose clothing

24. Which one of the wrenches pictured below is designed to grip round pipes in making plumbing repairs? 24._____

   A.    B.    C.    D.

25. Which one of the saws pictured below would be BEST to use to cut steel bar stock?   25._____

A.   B.   C.   D.

26. Which one of the hammers pictured below is a claw hammer?   26._____

A.   B.   C.   D.

27. The terms "dovetail" and "dowel" are used to describe types of   27._____

   A. glues   B. joints   C. clamps   D. tile

28. A three-prong plug on a power tool used on a 120-volt line indicates that the tool   28._____

   A. may be grounded against electric shock
   B. is provided with additional power through the third prong
   C. has a defect and should be returned
   D. is adaptable for use with AC or DC current

29. A bit and brace should be used to   29._____

   A. saw wood   B. glue wood
   C. drill holes   D. support or hold work

30. Which of the following would ordinarily occur FIRST in a toilet tank after the handle is pushed down to flush the toilet?   30._____

   A. Float ball drops with water level, opening the ballcock assembly through which fresh water flows into the tank
   B. Tank ball sinks slowly into place
   C. Rising water pushes the float ball up until it closes the ballcock assembly, shutting off the supply of fresh water when the tank is full
   D. The tank ball lifts, opening the outlet so water can flow from tank to bowl

KEY (CORRECT ANSWERS)

1.	C	16.	C
2.	A	17.	C
3.	D	18.	D
4.	D	19.	A
5.	B	20.	A
6.	A	21.	B
7.	C	22.	D
8.	C	23.	C
9.	D	24.	A
10.	B	25.	B
11.	D	26.	C
12.	A	27.	B
13.	B	28.	A
14.	D	29.	C
15.	B	30.	D

TEST 2

DIRECTIONS: Each question or incomplete statement is followed by several suggested answers or completions. Select the one that BEST answers the question or completes the statement. *PRINT THE LETTER OF THE CORRECT ANSWER IN THE SPACE AT THE RIGHT.*

1. Of the following, the MAIN reason for clear glass doors to have a painted design about four and one-half feet above the floor is to   1.____

   A. look attractive
   B. prevent glare
   C. improve safety
   D. make damage, if any, less noticeable

2. When using a wrench to make a repair on a faucet, it is a good idea to cover the wrench with rags in order to   2.____

   A. protect the finish on the faucet
   B. get a closer fit over the faucet
   C. get a better grip on the wrench
   D. get a better grip on the faucet

3. The length of the screw in the sketch below is *most nearly*   3.____

   A. 1 7/8"   B. 2"   C. 2 1/4"   D. 2 5/16"

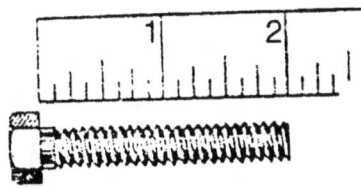

4. Panel doors may have horns which must be cut off before the door is hung. In the sketch below, the arrow which indicates a horn is labeled number   4.____

   A. 1   B. 2   C. 3   D. 4

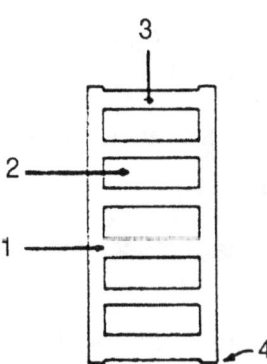

7

5. To "shim a hinge" means to

   A. swing the hinge from side to side
   B. paint the hinge
   C. polish the hinge
   D. raise up the hinge

6. To hold work that is being planed, sawed, drilled, shaped, sharpened or riveted, you should use a

   A. punch   B. rasp   C. reamer   D. vise

7. A good deal of the trouble caused by faulty and worn locks and hinges can be avoided by proper lubrication.
   The tool you would use to lubricate locks and hinges is

   A.   B.   C.   D.

8. The terms ALLIGATORING, BLISTERING, and PEELING refer to

   A. carpentry   B. masonry   C. painting   D. plumbing

9. The terms BAT and STRETCHER refer to

   A. carpentry   B. glazing   C. masonry   D. painting

10. Ladders which are used to extend as high as 60 feet are called

    A. extension ladders   B. portable ladders
    C. single-section ladders D. stepladders

11. Of the following, the MOST important advantage that Plexiglass has over regular glass, when used in windows, is that it

    A. is available in a wide range of thicknesses
    B. is easier to clean
    C. offers greater resistance to breakage
    D. offers greater resistance to scratches

12. Clutch-head, offset, Phillips and spiral-ratchet all are different types of

    A. drills   B. files   C. wrenches   D. screwdrivers

13. Of the following, the MOST important reason for keeping tools in perfect working order is to make sure

    A. the proper tool is being used for the required work
    B. the tools can be operated safely
    C. each employee can repair a variety of building defects
    D. no employee uses a tool for his private use

14. When repairing a hole in a leaking pipe which of the following should be done FIRST?   14.____

    A. Wrap tape around the hole
    B. Turn off the water supply
    C. Tighten a clamp around the hole
    D. Seal the hole with epoxy

15. Freshly cut threads on pipe should be handled with caution *mainly* because the threads   15.____

    A. are the weakest section of the pipe and break easily
    B. do not give a firm handhold for carrying
    C. make a tight seal around a joint
    D. are always sharp

16. When a repair worker must enter a confined space through a small opening, it is a GOOD idea to attach a rope to his body *mainly* because the   16.____

    A. rope reduces unnecessary strain on the body
    B. rope may provide a way to reach the worker in an emergency
    C. worker will be able to get to areas that are not easily reached
    D. worker may be able to use the rope to remove debris from the work space

17. Hitting the handle of a screw driver with a hammer to remove an imbedded screw is a   17.____

    A. *good* practice, since it supplies the necessary force to get the screw started
    B. *poor* practice, since the shank part of the screw driver can be bent and the tool made useless
    C. *good* practice, since hammers and screw drivers are available in every tool kit just for this purpose
    D. *poor* practice, since the blade tip of the screw driver cannot be guided into the screw slot when both hands are holding the tools

18. Of the following, the reason why a tank, such as that pictured below, that is otherwise working correctly might fail to fill up sufficiently to deliver enough water to the toilet bowl at the time it is needed is that the   18.____

    A. ball may not drop back over the valve seat
    B. excess water may be flowing into the drain
    C. float rod may be bent up
    D. valve seat may be worn or nicked

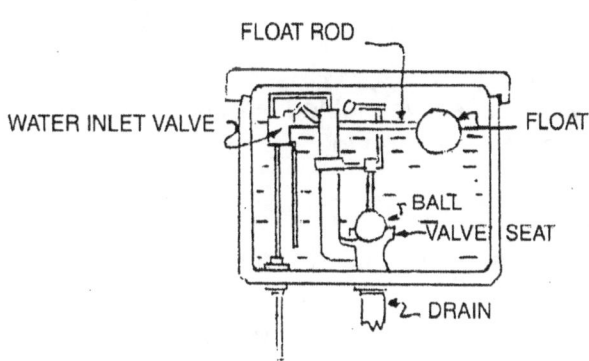

19. In the sketch below, the measurement of the inside diameter is *most nearly* _____ inches.

   A. 24 B. 3 C. 3 1/2 D. 4

20. In a two-wire electrical system, the color of the wire which is grounded is *usually*

   A. white B. red C. black D. green

21. It is generally recommended that wooden ladders be kept coated with a suitable protective coating.
   The one of the following which is NOT a suitable protective coating is

   A. clear lacquer B. clear varnish
   C. linseed oil D. paint

22. The tool you should use to mend metal by soldering is

   A. B. C. D.

23. Of the following, the MOST effective method of fixing a door that sticks is to locate the area of the door which sticks and then to _____ it.

   A. lacquer B. plane C. tape D. varnish

24. Which one of the following should be used to thin latex paint?

   A. Mineral spirits B. Turpentine
   C. Denatured alcohol D. Water

25. Of the following, the MAIN reason you should NOT place a ladder directly in front of a door that opens toward the ladder is that

    A. there is not enough space to support the weight of the ladder
    B. you would have to step down off the ladder each time someone wants to use the door
    C. this would prove to be hazardous if someone comes through the door
    D. it would be hard to reach the areas that need repair without tipping the ladder off balance

26. Going over the cutting line MORE than once when cutting a pane of glass by hand with a cutting wheel is *usually*

    A. *advisable;* it gives a straighter line
    B. *advisable;* it gives a cleaner break
    C. *inadvisable;* it gives an uneven break
    D. *inadvisable;* it may blunt the edge of the glass cutter

27. When hammering, it is usually BEST to hold the handle of the hammer

    A. close to the head because this maximizes the force of the blow
    B. far away from the head because this maximizes the force of the blow
    C. close to the head because this reduces the force of the blow
    D. far away from the head because this reduces the force of the blow

28. Repair crew members should report accidents on the job IMMEDIATELY *primarily* so that

    A. the proper person will be reprimanded for his carelessness
    B. a correct count can be kept of time lost through accidents
    C. prompt medical care may be given when needed
    D. the correct forms will be filled out

29. Leather gloves should be worn when handling sheet metal *primarily* because

    A. pressure on the metal might cause it to bend
    B. the edges and corners of the metal may be sharp
    C. natural oil or moisture from hands corrodes the metal
    D. leather provides a more secure grip

30. If a portable ladder does NOT have a nonslip base, the way to overcome this deficiency so that the ladder can be used safely is to

    A. place the ladder on soft earth
    B. fasten a wooden board across the top of the ladder
    C. splice two short ladders together
    D. tie the bottom of the ladder to a secure structure

KEY (CORRECT ANSWERS)

1.	C	16.	B
2.	A	17.	B
3.	B	18.	A
4.	D	19.	B
5.	D	20.	A
6.	D	21.	D
7.	B	22.	B
8.	C	23.	B
9.	C	24.	D
10.	A	25.	C
11.	C	26.	C
12.	D	27.	B
13.	B	28.	C
14.	B	29.	B
15.	D	30.	D

EXAMINATION SECTION
TEST 1

DIRECTIONS: Each question or incomplete statement is followed by several suggested answers or completions. Select the one that BEST answers the question or completes the statement. *PRINT THE LETTER OF THE CORRECT ANSWEE IN THE SPACE AT THE RIGHT.*

1. As a member of a repair crew, you have been asked by your supervisor to reinforce a door. You have never done this kind of work before and are not certain how to go about it. Of the following, the MOST advisable action to take is to

    A. tell your supervisor you need assistance
    B. ask the other crew members if they can help you
    C. go ahead and do the best you can
    D. ask another member of your crew if he will do it for you

    1.____

2. It is BEST to erect a barricade or barrier before repair work begins *mainly* because

    A. the repair truck can be sent back for additional supplies
    B. the workers can work in more comfortable space
    C. unauthorized persons are kept clear of the work area
    D. a solid platform is provided for workers' use

    2.____

3. Of the following, the BEST reason for sprinkling water on work areas which have a lot of dust or where the work itself will create a lot of dust is that this action will

    A. dissolve the dust particles
    B. help the dust to settle
    C. clean away the dust from the area
    D. prevent the dust from drying out

    3.____

QUESTIONS 4-9.

Questions 4 through 9 are to be answered *solely* on the basis of the following set of instructions.

Patching Simple Cracks in a Built-Up Roof

If there is a visible crack in built-up roofing, the repair is simple and straight forward:
1. With a brush, clean all loose gravel and dust out of the crack, and clean three or four inches around all sides of it.
2. With a trowel or putty knife, fill the crack with asphalt cement and then spread a layer of asphalt cement about 1/8 inch thick over the cleaned area.
3. Place a strip of roofing felt big enough to cover the crack into the wet cement and press it down firmly.
4. Spread a second layer of cement over the strip of felt and well past its edges.
5. Brush gravel back over the patch.

4. According to the above passage, in order to patch simple cracks in a built-up roof, it is necessary to use a

    A. putty knife and a drill B. knife and pliers
    C. tack hammer and a punch D. brush and a trowe

    4.____

13

5. According to the above passage, the size of the area that should be clear of loose gravel and dust before the asphalt cement is first applied should

   A. be the exact size of the crack itself
   B. extend three or four inches on all sides of the crack
   C. be 1/8 inch greater than the size of the crack itself
   D. extend the length of the roofing strip

6. According to the above passage, loose gravel and dust in the crack should be removed with a

   A. brush   B. felt pad   C. trowel   D. dust mop

7. Assume that both layers of asphalt cement needed to patch the crack are of the same thickness.
   The total thickness of asphalt cement used in the patch should be, *most nearly,* _____ inch.

   A. 1/2   B. 1/3   C. 1/4   D. 1/8

8. According to the instructions in the above passage, how large should the strip of roofing felt be cut?

   A. Three of four inches square
   B. Smaller than the crack and small enough to be surrounded by cement on all sides of the strip
   C. Exactly the same size and shape of the area covered by the wet cement
   D. Large enough to completely cover the crack

9. The final or finishing action to be taken in patching a simple crack in a built-up roof is to

   A. clean out the inside of the crack
   B. spread a layer of asphalt a second time
   C. cover the crack with roofing felt
   D. cover the patch of roofing felt and cement with gravel

10. As a repair crew worker, your supervisor tells you that he has in the workshop a piece of glass measuring 5' x 4' from which he wants you to cut a section measuring 4'8" x 3'2". However, you find two pieces of glass in the workshop; one is 5' x 3', and the other is 8' x 5'.
    Of the following, the BEST action for you to take is to

    A. cut a section measuring 4'8" x 3' from the smaller piece because that is probably what he meant
    B. do NOT cut the glass and wait until he asks you for it
    C. tell him about the differences in measurement and ask him what to do
    D. cut a section measuring 4'8" x 3'2" from the larger piece since that would give you the full size required

11. A floor that is 9' wide by 12' long measures how many square feet?

    A. 12   B. 21   C. 108   D. 150

12. The sum of 5 1/16, 4 1/4, 4 3/8, and 3 7/16 is 12.____

    A. 17 1/8   B. 17 7/16   C. 17 1/4   D. 17 3/8

13. From a length of pipe 6 feet 9 inches long you are asked to cut a piece 4 feet 5 inches 13.____
    long.
    The length of the remainder, in inches, should be

    A. 24   B. 26   C. 28   D. 53

QUESTIONS 14-17.
In answering questions 14 through 17 refer to the label pictured below.

LABEL

BREGSON'S CLEAR GLUE HIGHLY FLAMMABLE	PRECAUTIONS
A clear quick-drying glue	Use with adequate ventilation
For temporary bonding, apply glue to one surface and join immediately	Close container after use
For permanent bonding, apply glue to both surfaces, permit to dry and press together	Keep out of reach of children
Use for bonding plastic to plastic, plastic to wood, and wood to wood only	Avoid prolonged breathing of vapors and repeated contact with skin
Will not bond at temperatures below 60°	

14. Assume that you, as a member of a repair crew, have been asked to repair a wood banister in the hallway of a house. Since the heat has been turned off, the hallway is very cold, except for the location where you have to make the repair. Another repair crew worker is working at that same location using a blow torch to solder a pipe in the wall. 14.____

    The temperature at that location is about 67°.
    According to the instruction on the above label, the use of this glue to make the necessary repair is

    A. *advisable;* the glue will bond wood to wood
    B. *advisable;* the heat form the soldering will cause the glue to dry quickly
    C. *inadvisable;* the work area temperature is too low
    D. *inadvisable;* the glue is highly flammable

15. According to the instructions on the above label, this glue should NOT be used for which 15.____
    of the following applications?

    A. Affixing a pine table leg to a walnut table
    B. Repairing leaks around pipe joints
    C. Bonding a plastic knob to a cedar drawer
    D. Attaching a lucite knob to a lucite drawer

16. According to the instructions on the above label, using this glue to bond ceramic tile to a plaster wall by coating both surfaces with glue, letting the glue dry, and then pressing the tile to the plaster wall is

   A. *advisable;* the glue is quick drying and clear
   B. *advisable;* the glue should be permanently affixed to the one surface of the tile only
   C. *inadvisable;* the glue is not suitable for bonding ceramic tile to plaster walls
   D. *inadvisable;* the bonding should be a temporary one

17. The precaution described in the above label "use with adequate ventilation" means that

   A. the area you are working in should be very cold
   B. there should be sufficient fresh air where you are using the glue
   C. you should wear gloves to avoid contact with the glue
   D. you must apply a lot of glue to make a permanent bond

QUESTIONS 18-20.
Questions 18 through 20 are to be answered *solely* on the basis of the following passage.

A utility plan is a floor plan which shows the layout of a heating, electrical, plumbing, or other utility system. Utility plans are used primarily by the persons responsible for the utilities, but they are important to the craftsman as well. Most utility installations require the leaving of openings in walls, floors, and roofs for the admission or installation of utility features. The craftsman who is, for example, pouring a concrete foundation wall must study the utility plans to determine the number, sizes, and locations of the openings he must leave for piping, electric lines, and the like.

18. The one of the following items of information which is LEAST likely to be provided by a utility plan is the

   A. location of the joists and frame members around
   B. stairwells
   C. location of the hot water supply and return piping
   D. location of light fixtures D. number of openings in the floor for radiators

19. According to the passage, the persons who will *most likely* have the GREATEST need for the information included in a utility plan of a building are those who

   A. maintain and repair the heating system
   B. clean the premises
   C. paint housing exteriors
   D. advertise property for sale

20. According to the passage, a repair crew member should find it MOST helpful to consult a utility plan when information is needed about the

   A. thickness of all doors in the structure
   B. number of electrical outlets located throughout the structure
   C. dimensions of each window in the structure
   D. length of a roof rafter

KEY (CORRECT ANSWERS)

1. A
2. C
3. B
4. D
5. B

6. A
7. C
8. D
9. D
10. C

11. C
12. A
13. C
14. D
15. B

16. C
17. B
18. A
19. A
20. B

TEST 2

DIRECTIONS: Each question or incomplete statement is followed by several suggested answers or completions. Select the one that BEST answers the question or completes the statement. *PRINT THE LETTER OF THE CORRECT ANSWER IN THE SPACE AT THE RIGHT.*

1. Repair crew men should report accidents on the job IMMEDIATELY *primarily* so that   1.____

    A. the proper person will be reprimanded for his carelessness
    B. a correct count can be kept of time lost through accidents on the job
    C. prompt medical care may be given when needed
    D. the correct forms will be filled out

2. In a circulating hot-water heating system, most boilers have an altitude gauge that shows the level of the water in the system. This gauge has two needles, one red, which is set at the proper water level, and one black, which shows the true water level, and which varies with the water-level change. When the red needle is over the black on the gauge, so that they coincide, it means that the system   2.____

    A. has too much water
    B. requires more water
    C. is properly filled with water
    D. should be shut off

3. If a radiator fails to heat properly, the FIRST of the following actions which you should take is to check the   3.____

    A. boiler's steam gauge   B. boiler's water line
    C. radiator's shut-off valve   D. pressure reducing valve

4. Assume that you have been asked to remove a door knob. You inspect the door and find that it has a mortise lock, and that the door knob is fastened with a set screw.
Which of the following is the FIRST step that you should take in removing the door knob?   4.____

    A. Unscrew the set screw on the slimmest part of the knob
    B. Saw off the knob at its thinnest point
    C. Turn the knob repeatedly to the right and to the left until it finally falls off
    D. Use a pinchbar to spring the lock

5. When preparing a 1:1:6 mix for mortar, how many pails of lime should be added to 3 pails of sand and 1/2 pail of cement?   5.____

    A. 3   B. 1   C. 1/2   D. 1/4

6. If you find that the putty in the can is a little too hard to use, you should add some   6.____

    A. whiting   B. linseed oil
    C. spackle   D. glazing compound

7. The purpose of scratching the surface of the first coat of patching stucco is to 7.____

   A. spread the patching stucco over a wide area
   B. give the surface a textured finish
   C. provide a gripping surface for the next coat of patching stucco
   D. press the patching stucco into the hole to be repaired

8. When filling in large cracks and holes up to 2 inches in diameter in plaster walls it is BEST to use 8.____

   A. spackle
   B. patching plaster
   C. gypsum wallboard
   D. tile

9. Of the following, the MAIN reason for having a vertical distance of about 7 inches between stair treads is that this 9.____

   A. makes for the best appearance
   B. makes an easy step for the average person
   C. allows for the most profitable use of wood
   D. cuts out a good deal of unnecessary work

10. When removing a door from its hinges to make repairs, it is ALWAYS best to 10.____

    A. remove the pin from the top hinge first
    B. keep the door tightly closed
    C. remove the pin from the bottom hinge first
    D. remove the door knob and lock

11. Dry plaster will absorb water from the patching material, weakening and shrinking it. Based on the information in this statement, it would be *advisable* to take which one of the following actions in the process of patching a plaster crack? 11.____

    A. Mix the plaster with a lot of extra water
    B. Apply water-eased paint to the wall immediately
    C. Apply plaster powder to the crack, then pour water in over it
    D. Dampen the area surrounding the patch with a sponge

12. Standard electrical tools which are safe for ordinary use may be unsafe in locations which contain flammable materials because 12.____

    A. there may be insufficient ventilation
    B. sparks from the tools may start a fire
    C. electric current will usually cause fire
    D. the automatic sprinkler system may be set off accidentally

13. Of the following, the BEST combination of ingredients to use for good concrete is 13.____

    A. cement and water
    B. aggregate and water
    C. cement, sand, stone, and water
    D. gravel, cement, and water

14. If the blade of a screw driver is thicker than the slot at the top of a screw, the way to *properly* drive the screw into wood in this case is to

    A. widen the slot of the screw to fit the larger blade tip
    B. tap the end of the screw driver lightly to get a firmer hold into the screw slot
    C. get another screw driver which fits the size of the screw slot
    D. apply a drop of lubricating oil to the screw slot to get the screw started into the wood

14.____

QUESTIONS 15-20.
Questions 15 through 20 are to be answered *solely* on the basis of the following passage.

The basic hand-operated hoisting device is the tackle or purchase, consisting of a line called a fall, reeved through one or more blocks.

To hoist a load of given size, you must set up a rig with a safe working load equal to or in excess of the load to be hoisted. In order to do this, you must be able to calculate the safe working load of a single part of line of given size; the safe working load of a given purchase which contains a line of given size; and the minimum size of hooks or shackles which you must use in a given type of purchase to hoist a given load. You must also be able to calculate the thrust which a given load will exert on a gin pole or a set of shears inclined at a given angle; the safe working load which a spar of a given size, used as a gin pole or as one of a set of shears, will sustain; and the stress which a given load will set up in the back guy of a gin pole, or in the back guy of a set of shears, inclined at a given angle.

15. The above passage refers to the lifting of loads by means of

    A. erected scaffolds B. manual rigging devices
    C. power-driven equipment D. conveyor belts

15.____

16. It can be concluded from the above passage, that a set of shears serves to

    A. absorb the force and stress of the working load
    B. operate the tackle
    C. contain the working load
    D. compute the safe working load

16.____

17. According to the above passage, a spar can be used for a

    A. back guy   B. block   C. fall   D. gin pole

17.____

18. According to the above passage, the rule that a user of hand-operated tackle MUST follow is to make sure that the safe working load is at LEAST

    A. equal to the weight of the given load
    B. twice the combined weight of the block and falls
    C. one-half the weight of the given load
    D. twice the weight of the given load

18.____

19. According to the above passage, the two parts that make up a tackle are

    A. back guys and gin poles B. blocksm and falls
    C. rigs and shears D. spars and shackles

19.____

20. According to the above passage, in order to determine whether it is safe to hoist a particular load, you MUST
    A. use the maximum size hooks
    B. time the speed to bring a given load to a desired place
    C. calculate the forces exerted on various types of rigs
    D. repeatedly lift and lower various loads

20.____

KEY (CORRECT ANSWERS)

1.	C	11.	D
2.	C	12.	B
3.	C	13.	C
4.	A	14.	C
5.	C	15.	B
6.	B	16.	A
7.	C	17.	D
8.	B	18.	A
9.	B	19.	B
10.	C	20.	C

EXAMINATION SECTION
TEST 1

DIRECTIONS: Each question or incomplete statement is followed by several suggested answers or completions. Select the one that BEST answers the question or completes the statement. *PRINT THE LETTER OF THE CORRECT ANSWER IN THE SPACE AT THE RIGHT.*

1. Linseed oil putty would MOST likely be used to secure glass in _____ windows. 1._____

    A. steel casement
    B. aluminum jalousie
    C. wood double hung
    D. aluminum storm

2. Of the following, the one type of glass that should NOT be cut with the ordinary type glass cutter is _____ glass. 2._____

    A. safety   B. plate   C. wire   D. herculite

3. Thermopane is made of two sheets of glass separated by 3._____

    A. a sheet of celluloid
    B. wire mesh
    C. an air space
    D. mica

4. Glass is NEVER cut so that it fits snugly inside the frame of a steel casement window. Of the following, the MAIN reason for allowing this space between the glass and the side of the frame is to 4._____

    A. prevent cracking of the glass in cold weather
    B. permit the glass to be lined up properly
    C. allow space for the putty
    D. eliminate the necessity of polishing the edges of the glass

5. Glass is held in steel sash by means of 5._____

    A. points   B. clips   C. plates   D. blocks

6. When nailing felt to a roof, the nails should be driven through a 6._____

    A. tinned disc
    B. steel washer
    C. brass plate
    D. plastic bushing

7. An opening in a parapet wall for draining water from a roof is MOST often called a 7._____

    A. leader   B. gutter   C. downspout   D. scupper

8. Roofing nails are usually 8._____

    A. brass
    B. cement coated
    C. galvanized
    D. nickel plated

9. A *street ell* is a fitting having 9._____

    A. male threads at both ends
    B. male threads at one end and female threads at the other end
    C. female threads at both ends
    D. male threads at one end and a solder connection at the other end

10. Of the following pieces of equipment, the one on which you would MOST likely find a safety (pop-off) valve is a(n)

    A. hot air furnace
    B. air conditioning compressor
    C. hot water heater
    D. dehumidifier

11. Compression fittings are MOST often used with

    A. cast iron bell and spigot pipe
    B. steel flange pipe
    C. copper tubing
    D. transite

12. Water hammer is BEST eliminated by

    A. increasing the size of all the piping
    B. installing an air chamber
    C. replacing the valve seats with neoprene gaskets
    D. flushing the system to remove corrosion

13. The BEST type of pipe to use in a gas line in a domestic installation is

    A. black iron   B. galvanized iron
    C. cast iron   D. wrought steel

14. If there is a pinhole in the float of a toilet tank, the

    A. water will flush continually
    B. toilet cannot flush
    C. tank cannot be filled with water
    D. valve will not shut off so water will overflow into the overflow tube

15. Condensation of moisture in humid weather occurs MOST often on _____ pipe(s).

    A. sewage   B. gas
    C. hot water   D. cold water

16. A gas appliance should be connected to a gas line by means of a(n)

    A. union   B. right and left coupling
    C. elbow   D. close nipple

17. A PRINCIPAL difference between a pipe thread and a machine thread is that the pipe thread is

    A. tapered   B. finer   C. flat   D. longer

18. When joining galvanized iron pipe, pipe joint compound is placed on

    A. the female threads only
    B. the male threads only
    C. both the male and female threads
    D. either the male or the female threads depending on the type of fitting

19. If moisture is trapped between the layers of a 3-ply roof, the heat of a summer day will

    A. dry the roof out
    B. cause blisters to be formed in the roofing
    C. rot the felt material
    D. have no effect on the roofing

20. Of the following, the metal MOST often used for leaders and gutters is

    A. monel
    B. brass
    C. steel
    D. galvanized iron

21. When drilling a small hole in sheet copper, the BEST practice is to

    A. make a dent with a center punch first
    B. put some cutting oil at the point you intend to drill
    C. use a slow speed drill to prevent overheating
    D. use an auger type bit

22. The reason for annealing sheet copper is to make it

    A. soft and easier to work
    B. more resistant to weather
    C. easier to solder
    D. harder and more resistant to blows

23. In draw filing,

    A. only the edge of the file is used
    B. a triangle file is generally used
    C. the file is pulled toward the mechanic's body in filing
    D. the file must have a safe edge

24. The type of paint that uses water as a thinner is

    A. enamel   B. latex   C. shellac   D. lacquer

25. The reason for placing a 6" sub-base of cinders under a concrete sidewalk is to

    A. provide flexibility in the surface
    B. permit drainage of water
    C. prevent chemicals in the soil from damaging the sidewalk
    D. allow room for the concrete to expand

26. The BEST material to use to lubricate a door lock is

    A. penetrating oil
    B. pike oil
    C. graphite
    D. light grease

27. Assume that the color of the flame from a gas stove is bright yellow. To correct this, you should

    A. close the air flap
    B. open the air flap
    C. increase the gas pressure
    D. increase the size of the gas opening

28. In a 110-220 volt three-wire circuit, the neutral wire is usually

   A. black   B. red   C. white   D. green

29. Brushes on fractional horsepower universal motors are MOST often made of

   A. flexible copper strands
   B. rigid carbon blocks
   C. thin wire strips
   D. collector rings

30. Leaks from the stem of a faucet can generally be stopped by replacing the

   A. bibb washer   B. seat   C. packing   D. gasket

31. Of the following, the BEST procedure to follow with a frozen water pipe is to

   A. allow the pipe to thaw out by itself as the weather gets warmer
   B. put anti-freeze into the pipe above the section that is frozen
   C. turn on the hot water heater
   D. open the faucet closest to the frozen pipe and warm the pipe with a blow torch, starting at this point

32. The one of the following that is NOT usually changed by a central air conditioning system is the

   A. volume of air in the system
   B. humidity of the air
   C. dust in the air
   D. air pressure of the system

33. The temperature of a domestic hot water system is MOST often controlled by a(n)

   A. relief valve   B. aquastat   C. barometer   D. thermostat

34. Draft in a chimney is MOST often controlled by a(n)

   A. damper
   B. gate
   C. orifice
   D. cross connection

35. Assume that a refrigerator motor operates continuously for excessively long periods of time.
The FIRST item you should check to locate the defect is the

   A. plug in the outlet
   B. door gasket
   C. direction of rotation of the motor
   D. motor switch

36. Assume that after replacing a defective motor for a large electric fan, you find that the fan is rotating in the wrong direction.
If the motor is a split phase motor, with the shaft at one end only, the trouble could be CORRECTED by

   A. reversing the fan on its shaft
   B. turning the motor end for end
   C. interchanging the connections on the field terminals of the motor
   D. reversing the plug in the electric outlet

37. In order to properly hang a door, shims are frequently inserted under the hinges. These shims are MOST often made of

   A. cardboard
   B. sheet steel
   C. bakelite
   D. the same materials as the hinges

38. Flooring nails are usually _____ nails.

   A. casing   B. common   C. cut   D. clinch

39. Over a doorway, to support brick, you will usually find

   A. steel angles   B. hanger bolts
   C. wooden headers   D. stirrups

40. Insulation of steam pipes is MOST often done with

   A. asbestos   B. celotex   C. alundum   D. sheathing

41. Assume that only the first few coils of a hot water convector used for heating a room are hot.
    To correct this, you should FIRST

   A. increase the water pressure
   B. increase the water temperature
   C. bleed the air out of the convector
   D. clean the convector pipes

42. The MAIN reason for grounding the outer sheel of an electric fixture is to

   A. provide additional support for the fixture
   B. reduce the cost of installation of the fixture
   C. provide a terminal to which the wires can be attached
   D. reduce the chance of electric shock

43. In woodwork, countersinking is MOST often done for

   A. lag screws   B. carriage bolts
   C. hanger bolts   D. flat head screws

44. Bridging is MOST often used in connection with

   A. door frames   B. window openings
   C. floor joists   D. stud walls

45. A saddle is part of a

   A. doorway   B. window
   C. stair well   D. bulkhead

46. To make it easier to drive screws into hard wood, it is BEST to   46.____

    A. use a screwdriver that is longer than that used for soft wood
    B. rub the threads of the screw on a bar of soap
    C. oil the screw threads
    D. use a square shank screwdriver assisted by a wrench

47. In using a doweled joint to make a repair of a wooden door, it is important to remember   47.____
    that the dowel

    A. hole must be smaller in diameter than the dowel so that there is a tight fit
    B. hole must be longer than the dowel to provide a room for excess glue
    C. must be of the same type of wood as the door frame
    D. must be held in place by a small screw while waiting for the glue to set

48. The edges of MOST finished wood flooring are   48.____

    A. tongue and groove   B. mortise and tenon
    C. bevel and miter   D. lap and scarf

49. For the SMOOTHEST finish, sanding of wood should be done   49.____

    A. in a circular direction
    B. diagonally against the grain
    C. across the grain
    D. parallel with the grain

50. To prevent splintering of wood when boring a hole through it, the BEST practice is to   50.____

    A. drill at a slow speed
    B. use a scrap piece to back up the work
    C. use an auger bit
    D. ease up the pressure on the drill when the drill is almost through the wood

KEY (CORRECT ANSWERS)

1. C	11. C	21. A	31. D	41. C
2. D	12. B	22. A	32. D	42. D
3. C	13. A	23. C	33. B	43. D
4. A	14. D	24. B	34. A	44. C
5. B	15. D	25. B	35. B	45. A
6. A	16. B	26. C	36. C	46. B
7. D	17. A	27. B	37. A	47. B
8. C	18. B	28. C	38. C	48. A
9. B	19. B	29. B	39. A	49. D
10. C	20. D	30. C	40. A	50. B

TEST 2

DIRECTIONS: Each question or incomplete statement is followed by several suggested answers or completions. Select the one that BEST answers the question or completes the statement. *PRINT THE LETTER OF THE CORRECT ANSWER IN THE SPACE AT THE RIGHT.*

1. A *speed nut* has

   A. no threads
   B. threads that are coarser than a standard nut
   C. threads that are finer than s standard nut
   D. fewer threads than a standard nut

2. The BEST tool to use to remove the burr and sharp edge resulting from cutting tubing with a tube cutter is a

   A. file   B. scraper   C. reamer   D. knife

3. A router is used PRINCIPALLY to

   A. clean pipe
   B. cut grooves in wood
   C. bend electric conduit
   D. sharpen tools

4. The principle of operation of a sabre saw is MOST similar to that of a _____ saw.

   A. circular   B. radial   C. swing   D. jig

5. A full thread cutting set would have both taps and

   A. cutters   B. bushings   C. dies   D. plugs

6. The proper flux to use for soldering electric wire connections is

   A. rosin
   B. killed acid
   C. borax
   D. zinc chloride

7. A fusestat differs from an ordinary plug fuse in that a fusestat has

   A. less current carrying capacity
   B. different size threads
   C. an aluminum shell instead of a copper shell
   D. no threads

8. A grounding type 120-volt receptacle differs from an ordinary electric receptacle MAINLY in that a grounding receptacle

   A. is larger than the ordinary receptacle
   B. has openings for a three prong plug
   C. can be used for larger machinery
   D. has a built-in circuit breaker

9. A carbide tip is MOST often found on a bit used for drilling

   A. concrete   B. wood   C. steel   D. brass

10. The MAIN reason for using oil on an oilstone is to

    A. make the surface of the stone smoother
    B. prevent clogging of the pores of the stone
    C. reduce the number of times the stone has to be *dressed*
    D. prevent gouging of the stone's surface

11. The sum of the following numbers, 1 3/4, 3 1/6, 5 1/2, 6 5/8, and 9 1/4, is

    A. 26 1/8   B. 26 1/4   C. 26 1/2   D. 26 3/4

12. If a piece of plywood measures 5' 1 1/4" x 3' 2 1/2", the number of square feet in this board is MOST NEARLY

    A. 15.8   B. 16.1   C. 16.4   D. 16.7

13. Assume that in quantity purchases the city receives a discount of 33 1/3%.
    If a one gallon can of paint retails at $5.33 per gallon, the cost of 375 gallons of this paint is MOST NEARLY

    A. $1,332.50   B. $1,332.75   C. $1,333.00   D. $1,333.25

14. Assume that eight barrels of cement together weigh a total of 3004 lbs. and 12 oz.
    If there are four bags of cement per barrel, then the weight of one bag of cement is MOST NEARLY _____ lbs.

    A. 93.1   B. 93.5   C. 93.9   D. 94.3

15. Assume that one man cuts 50 nameplates per hour, whereas his co-worker cuts 55 nameplates per hour.
    At the end of 7 hours, the first man will have cut fewer nameplates than the second man by

    A. 9.3%   B. 9.5%   C. 9.7%   D. 9.9%

16. Under the same conditions, the one of the following that dries the FASTEST is

    A. shellac   B. varnish   C. enamel   D. lacquer

17. Interior wood trim in a building is MOST often made of

    A. hemlock   B. pine   C. cedar   D. oak

18. Gaskets are seldom made of

    A. rubber   B. lead   C. asbestos   D. vinyl

19. Toggle bolts are MOST frequently used to

    A. fasten shelf supports to a hollow block wall
    B. fasten furniture legs to table tops
    C. anchor machinery to a concrete floor
    D. join two pieces of sheet metal

20. Rubber will deteriorate FASTEST when it is constantly in contact with

    A. air   B. water   C. oil   D. soapsuds

21. Stoppage of water flow is often caused by dirt <u>accumulating</u> in an elbow. 21._____
    As used in the above sentence, the word <u>accumulating</u> means MOST NEARLY

    A. clogging   B. collecting   C. rusting   D. confined

22. The surface of the metal was <u>embossed</u>. 22._____
    As used in the above sentence, the word <u>embossed</u> means MOST NEARLY

    A. polished   B. rough   C. raised   D. painted

Questions 23-24.

DIRECTIONS: Questions 23 and 24 are to be answered in accordance with the following paragraph.

When fixing an upper sash cord, you must also remove the lower sash. To do this, the parting strip between the sash must be removed. Now remove the cover from the weight box channel, cut off the cord as before, and pull it over the pulleys. Pull your new cord over the pulleys and down into the channel, where it may be fastened to the weight. The cord for an upper sash is cut off 1" or 2" below the pulley with the weight resting on the floor of the pocket and the cord held taut. These measurements allow for slight stretching of the cord. When the cord is cut to length, it can be pulled up over the pulley and tied with a single common knot in the end to fit into the socket in the sash groove. If the knot protrudes beyond the face of the sash, tap it gently to flatten. In this way, it will not become frayed from constant rubbing against the groove.

23. When repairing the upper sash cord, the FIRST thing to do is to 23._____

    A. remove the lower sash
    B. cut the existing sash cord
    C. remove the parting strip
    D. measure the length of new cord necessary

24. According to the above paragraph, the rope may become frayed if the 24._____

    A. pulley is too small   B. knot sticks out
    C. cord is too long   D. weight is too heavy

25. In the repair of the sash cord mentioned in the paragraph for Questions 23 and 24, the MAIN reason for cutting off the sash cord below the bottom of the pulley is to 25._____

    A. prevent the cord from tangling
    B. save on amount of cord used
    C. prevent the sash weight from hitting the bottom of the frame in use
    D. provide room for tying the knot

26. Of the following drawings, the one that would be considered an *elevation* of a building is the 26._____

    A. floor plan   B. front view   C. cross section   D. site plan

27. On a plan, the symbol shown at the right USUALLY represents a(n) 27._____

    A. duplex receptacle   B. electric switch
    C. ceiling outlet   D. pull box

28. On a plan, the symbol _____ - _____ - USUALLY represents a

    A. center line
    B. hidden outline
    C. long break
    D. dimension line

29. Assume that on a plan you see the following: 1/4" - 20 NC-2. This refers to the

    A. diameter of a hole
    B. size and type of screw thread
    C. taper of a pin
    D. scale at which the plan is drawn

30. In reference to the above sketch, the length of the diagonal part of the plate indicated by the question mark is MOST NEARLY

    A. 13"   B. 14"   C. 15"   D. 16"

31. To increase the workability of concrete without changing its strength, the BEST procedure to follow is to increase the percentage of

    A. water
    B. cement and sand
    C. cement and water
    D. water and sand

32. The MAIN reason for covering freshly poured concrete with tar paper is to

    A. prevent evaporation of water
    B. stop people from walking on the concrete
    C. protect the concrete from rain
    D. keep back any earth that may fall on the concrete

33. The MAIN reason for using air-entrained cement in sidewalks is to

    A. protect the concrete from the effects of freezing
    B. color the concrete
    C. speed up the setting time of the concrete
    D. make the concrete more workable

34. Assume that a reinforcing bar used for concrete is badly rusted.
Before using this bar,

   A. it is not necessary to remove any rust
   B. only loose rust need be removed
   C. all rust should be removed
   D. all rust should be removed and a coat of red lead paint is applied

35. Assume that freshly poured concrete has been exposed to freezing temperatures for 6 hours.
In all likelihood, this concrete

   A. has been permanently damaged
   B. will harden properly as soon as the air temperature warms up
   C. will harden properly even though the temperature remains below freezing
   D. will eventually harden properly, but it will take much longer than usual

36. Assume that concrete for a floor in a play yard is to be placed directly on the earth. On checking, you find that, because of a recent rain, the earth is damp.
You should

   A. wait till the sun dries the earth before placing the concrete
   B. use a waterproofing material between the concrete slab and the earth
   C. use less water in the concrete mix
   D. ignore the damp earth and place the concrete as you normally would

37. The MAJOR disadvantage of *floating* the surface of concrete too much is that the

   A. surface will become too rough
   B. surface will become weak and will wear rapidly
   C. initial set will be disturbed
   D. concrete cannot be cured properly

38. In addition to water and sand, mortar mix for a cinder block wall is usually made of

   A. gravel and lime
   B. plaster and cement
   C. gravel and cement
   D. lime and cement

39. The *nominal* size of a standard cinder block is

   A. 8" x 6" x 16"
   B. 8" x 8" x 16"
   C. 8" x 12" x 12"
   D. 6" x 8" x 12"

40. The *bond* of a brick wall refers to the

   A. arrangement of headers and stretchers
   B. time it takes for the mortar to set
   C. way a brick wall is tied in to an intersecting wall
   D. type of mortar used in the wall

41. The purpose of *tooling* when erecting a brick wall is to

   A. cut the brick to fit into a small space
   B. insure that the brick is laid level
   C. compact the mortar at the joints
   D. hold the brick in place till the mortar sets

42. Mortar is BEST cleaned off the face of a brick wall by using

   A. muriatic acid
   B. lye
   C. oxalic acid
   D. sodium hypochlorite

43. A brick wall is *pointed* to

   A. make sure it is the correct height
   B. repair the mortar joints
   C. set the brick in place
   D. arrange the mortar bed before setting the brick

44. The second coat in a three-coat plaster job is the _____ coat.

   A. scratch   B. brown   C. putty   D. lime

45. To repair fine cracks in a plastered wall, the PROPER material to use is

   A. lime
   B. cement wash
   C. perlite
   D. spackle

46. Gypsum lath for plastering is purchased in

   A. strips 5/16" x 1 1/2" x 4'
   B. rolls 3/8" x 48" x 96"
   C. boards 1/2" x 16" x 48"
   D. sheets 5/16" x 27" x 96"

47. The PRINCIPAL reason for using acoustic tile instead of ordinary tile is that the acoustic tile

   A. deadens sound
   B. is easier to apply
   C. is longer lasting
   D. costs less

48. The MAXIMUM thickness of the finish coat of white plaster is MOST NEARLY

   A. 1/8"   B. 1/4"   C. 3/8"   D. 1/2"

49. When using tape to conceal joints in dry wall construction, the FIRST operation is

   A. channelling the grooves between boards
   B. applying cement to the joints
   C. sanding the edges of the joints
   D. packing the tape into the joints

50. For the FIRST coat of plaster on wire lath, plaster of paris is mixed with

   A. cement   B. sand   C. lime   D. mortar

KEY (CORRECT ANSWERS)

1. A	11. B	21. B	31. C	41. C
2. C	12. C	22. C	32. A	42. A
3. B	13. A	23. C	33. A	43. B
4. D	14. C	24. B	34. B	44. B
5. C	15. D	25. C	35. A	45. D
6. A	16. D	26. B	36. D	46. C
7. B	17. B	27. C	37. B	47. A
8. B	18. D	28. A	38. D	48. A
9. A	19. A	29. B	39. B	49. B
10. B	20. C	30. A	40. A	50. B

EXAMINATION SECTION
TEST 1

DIRECTIONS: Each question or incomplete statement is followed by several suggested answers or completions. Select the one that BEST answers the question or completes the statement. *PRINT THE LETTER OF THE CORRECT ANSWER IN THE SPACE AT THE RIGHT.*

1.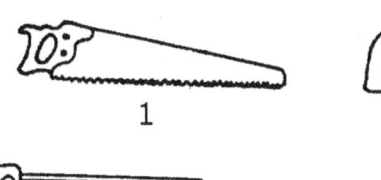

   The saw that is used PRINCIPALLY where curved cuts are to be made is numbered

   A. 1 B. 2 C. 3 D. 4

2.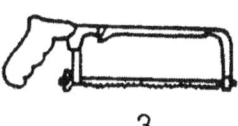

   The wrench that is used PRINCIPALLY for pipe work is numbered

   A. 1 B. 2 C. 3 D. 4

3.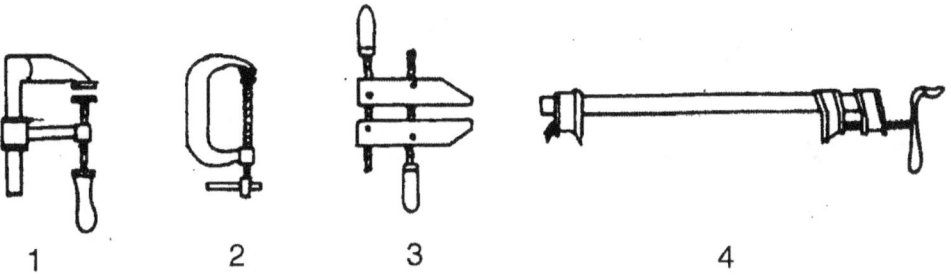

   The carpenter's *hand screw* is numbered

   A. 1 B. 2 C. 3 D. 4

4.

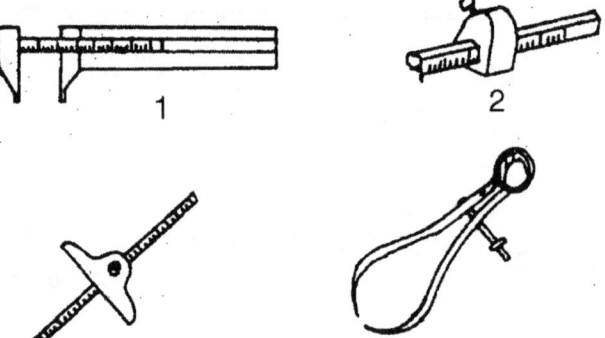

The tool used to measure the depth of a hole is numbered

A. 1   B. 2   C. 3   D. 4

5.

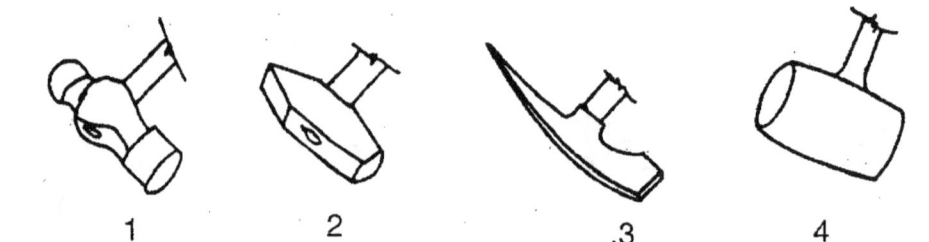

The tool that is BEST suited for use with a wood chisel is numbered

A. 1   B. 2   C. 3   D. 4

6.

The screw head that would be tightened with an *Allen* wrench is numbered

A. 1   B. 2   C. 3   D. 4

7.

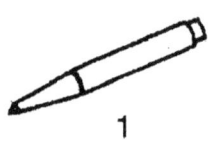  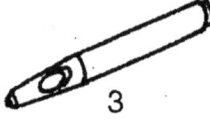

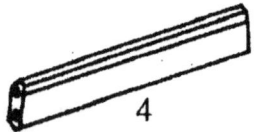

The center punch is numbered

A. 1   B. 2   C. 3   D. 4

8.

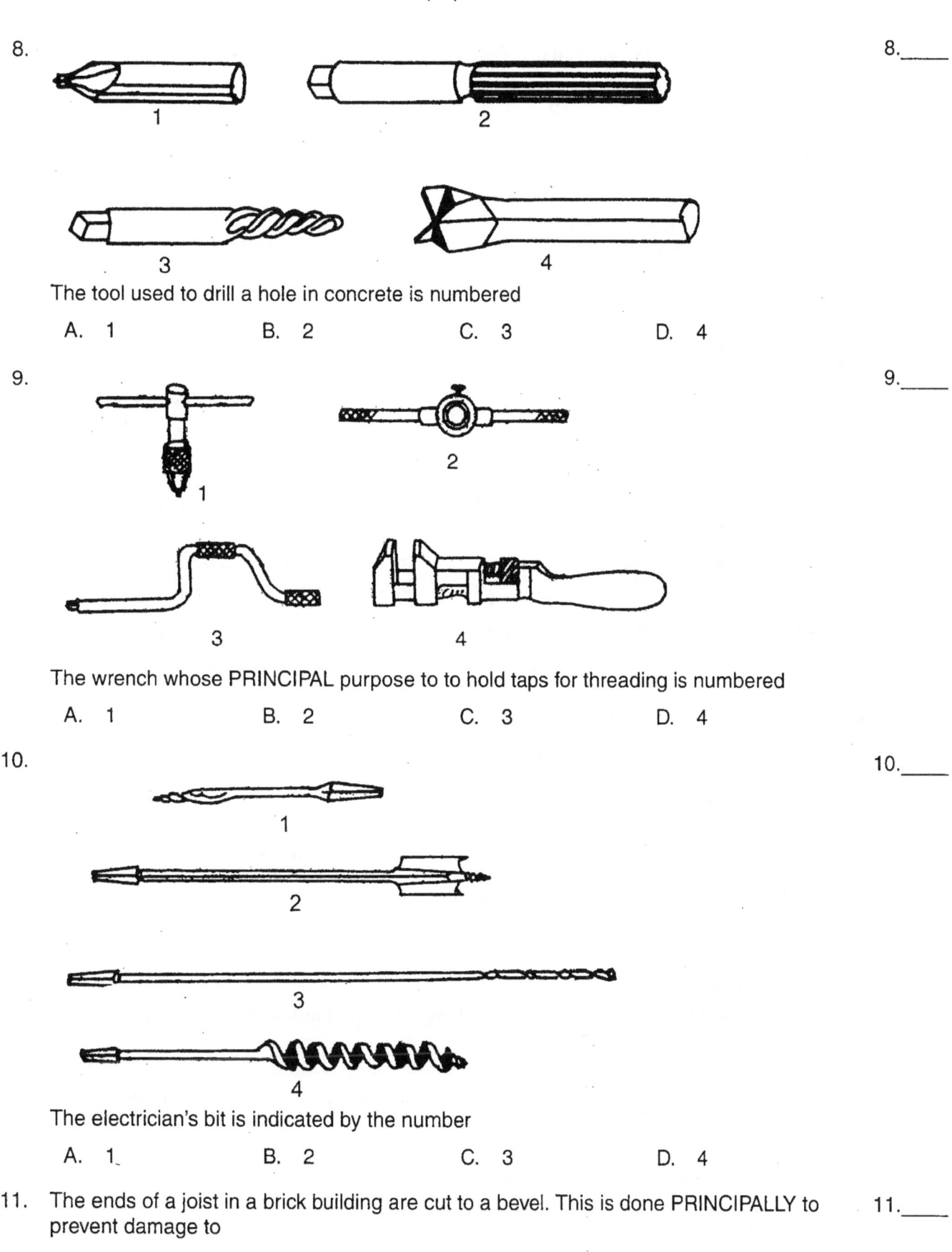

The tool used to drill a hole in concrete is numbered

   A. 1   B. 2   C. 3   D. 4

9.

The wrench whose PRINCIPAL purpose to to hold taps for threading is numbered

   A. 1   B. 2   C. 3   D. 4

10.

The electrician's bit is indicated by the number

   A. 1   B. 2   C. 3   D. 4

11. The ends of a joist in a brick building are cut to a bevel. This is done PRINCIPALLY to prevent damage to

   A. joist   B. floor   C. sill   D. wall

12. Of the following, the wood that is MOST commonly used today for floor joists is 12._____

    A. long leaf yellow pine B. douglas fir
    C. oak D. birch

13. Quarter-sawed lumber is preferred for the BEST finished flooring PRINCIPALLY because it 13._____

    A. has the greatest strength B. shrinks the least
    C. is the easiest to nail D. is the easiest to handle

14. A tool used in hanging doors is a 14._____

    A. miter gauge B. line level
    C. try square D. butt gauge

15. Of the following, the MAXIMUM height that would be considered acceptable for a stair riser is 15._____

    A. 6 1/2" B. 7 1/2" C. 8 1/2" D. 9 1/2"

16. The PRINCIPAL reason for *cross banding* the layers of wood in a plywood panel is to _____ of the panel. 16._____

    A. reduce warping B. increase the strength
    C. reduce the cost D. increase the beauty

17. The part of a tree that will produce the DENSEST wood is the _____ wood. 17._____

    A. spring B. summer C. sap D. heart

18. Casing nails MOST NEARLY resemble _____ nails. 18._____

    A. common B. roofing C. form D. finishing

19. Lumber in quantity is ordered by 19._____

    A. cubic feet B. foot board measure
    C. lineal feet D. weight and length

20. For finishing of wood, BEST results are obtained by sanding 20._____

    A. with a circular motion
    B. against the grain
    C. with the grain
    D. with a circular motion on edges and against the grain on the flat parts

21. A *chase* in a brick wall is a 21._____

    A. pilaster B. waterstop C. recess D. corbel

22. Parging refers to 22._____

    A. increasing the thickness of a brick wall
    B. plastering the back of face brickwork
    C. bonding face brick to backing blocks
    D. leveling each course of brick

23. The PRINCIPAL reason for requiring brick to be wetted before laying is that   23.____

    A. less water is required in the mortar
    B. efflorescence is prevented
    C. the brick will not absorb as much water from the mortar
    D. cool brick is easier to handle

24. In brickwork, muriatic acid is commonly used to   24.____

    A. increase the strength of the mortar
    B. etch the brick
    C. waterproof the wall
    D. clean the wall

25. Cement mortar can be made easier to work by the addition of a small quantity of   25.____

    A. lime   B. soda   C. litharge   D. plaster

26. Headers in brickwork are used to _____ the wall.   26.____

    A. strengthen   B. reduce the cost of
    C. speed the erection of   D. align

27. Joints in brick walls are tooled   27.____

    A. immediately after each brick is laid
    B. after the mortar has had its initial set
    C. after the entire wall is completed
    D. 28 days after the wall has been built

28. If cement mortar has begun to set before it can be used in a wall, the BEST thing to do is to   28.____

    A. use the mortar immediately as is
    B. add a small quantity of lime
    C. add some water and mix thoroughly
    D. discard the mortar

29. A *bat* in brickwork is a   29.____

    A. brace to hold a wall temporarily in place
    B. stick used to aid in mixing of mortar
    C. broken piece of brick used to fill short spaces
    D. curved brick used in ornamental work

30. The proportions by volume of cement, lime, and sand in a cement-lime mortar should be, according to the Building Code,   30.____

    A. 1:1:3   B. 2:1:6   C. 1:1:6   D. 1:2:6

31. The BEST flux to use when soldering galvanized iron is   31.____

    A. killed acid   B. sal-ammoniac
    C. muriatic acid   D. resin

32. When soldering a vertical joint, the soldering iron should be tinned on _____ side(s).   32.____
    A. 1   B. 2   C. 3   D. 4

33. The difference between *right hand* and *left hand* tin snips is the   33.____
    A. relative position of the cutting jaws
    B. shape of the cutting jaws
    C. shape of the handles
    D. relative position of the handles

34. A machine used to bend sheet metal is called a   34.____
    A. router   B. planer   C. brake   D. swage

35. The type of solder that would be used in *hard soldering* would be _____ solder.   35.____
    A. bismuth   B. wiping   C. 50-50   D. silver

36. Roll roofing material is usually felt which has been impregnated with   36.____
    A. cement   B. mastic   C. tar   D. latex

37. The purpose of flashing on roofs is to   37.____
    A. secure roofing materials to the roof
    B. make it easier to lay the roofing
    C. prevent leaks through the roof
    D. insulate the roof from excessive heat

38. The tool used to spread hot pitch on a three-ply roofing job is a   38.____
    A. mop   B. spreader   C. pusher   D. broom

39. The cutting of glass can be facilitated by dipping the cutting wheel in   39.____
    A. *3-in-1* oil   B. water   C. lard   D. kerosene

40. The strips of metal used to hold glass to the window frame while it is being puttied are called   40.____
    A. hold-downs B. points   C. wedges   D. triangles

41. The type of chain used with sash weights is _____ link.   41.____
    A. flat   B. round
    C. figure-eight   D. basket-weave

42. The material that would be used to seal around a window frame is   42.____
    A. oakum   B. litharge   C. grout   D. calking

43. The function of a window sill is MOST NEARLY the same as that of a   43.____
    A. jamb   B. coping   C. lintel   D. brick

44. Lightweight plaster would be made with   44.____
    A. sand   B. cinders   C. potash   D. vermiculite

45. The FIRST coat of plaster to be applied on a three-coat plaster job is the _____ coat.

    A. brown   B. scratch   C. white   D. keene

46. Screeds in plaster work are used to

    A. remove larger sizes of sand
    B. hold the batch of plaster before it is applied
    C. apply the plaster to the wall
    D. guide the plasterer in making, an even wall

47. The FIRST coat of plaster over rock lath should be a _____ plaster.

    A. gypsum
    B. lime
    C. portland cement
    D. puzzolan cement

48. In plastering, a *hawk* is used to _____ plaster.

    A. apply   B. hold   C. scratch   D. smooth

49. When mixing concrete by hand, the order in which the ingredients should be mixed is:

    A. water, cement, sand, stone
    B. sand, cement, water, stone
    C. stone, water, sand, cement
    D. stone, sand, cement, water

50. The PRINCIPAL reason for covering a concrete sidewalk with straw or paper after the concrete has been poured is to

    A. prevent people from walking on the concrete while it is still wet
    B. impart a rough non-slip surface to the concrete
    C. prevent excessive evaporation of water in the concrete
    D. shorten the length of time it would take for the concrete to harden

KEY (CORRECT ANSWERS)

1. B	11. D	21. C	31. C	41. A
2. B	12. B	22. B	32. A	42. D
3. C	13. B	23. C	33. A	43. B
4. C	14. D	24. D	34. C	44. D
5. D	15. B	25. A	35. D	45. B
6. C	16. A	26. A	36. C	46. D
7. A	17. D	27. B	37. C	47. A
8. D	18. D	28. D	38. A	48. B
9. A	19. B	29. C	39. D	49. D
10. C	20. C	30. C	40. B	50. C

TEST 2

DIRECTIONS: Each question or incomplete statement is followed by several suggested answers or completions. Select the one that BEST answers the question or completes the statement. *PRINT THE LETTER OF THE CORRECT ANSWER IN THE SPACE AT THE RIGHT.*

1. When colored concrete is required, the colors used should be 1.____
    A. colors in oil
    B. mineral pigments
    C. tempera colors
    D. water colors

2. Concrete is *rubbed* with a(n) 2.____
    A. emery wheel
    B. carborundum brick
    C. sandstone
    D. alundum stick

3. To prevent concrete from sticking to forms, the forms should be painted with 3.____
    A. oil   B. kerosene   C. water   D. lime

4. The reinforcement in a concrete floor slab is referred to as 6"-6" x #6-#6. The type of reinforcing that is being used is 4.____
    A. steel bars
    B. wire mesh
    C. angle irons
    D. grating plate

5. One method of measuring the consistency of a concrete mix is by means of a _____ test. 5.____
    A. penetration   B. flow   C. slump   D. weight

6. A chemical that is sometimes used to prevent the freezing of concrete in cold weather is 6.____
    A. alum
    B. glycerine
    C. calcium chloride
    D. sodium nitrate

7. The one of the following that is LEAST commonly used for columns is 7.____
    A. wide flange beams
    B. angles
    C. concrete-filled pipe
    D. *I* beams

8. Fire protection of steel floor beams is MOST frequently accomplished by the use of 8.____
    A. gypsum block
    B. brick
    C. rock wool fill
    D. vermiculite gypsum plaster

9. A *Pittsburgh lock* is a(n) 9.____
    A. emergency door lock
    B. sheet metal joint
    C. elevator safety
    D. boiler valve

10. In order to drill a hole at right angle to the horizontal axis of a round bar, the bar should be held in a 10.____
    A. step block
    B. C-block
    C. hand pliers
    D. V-block

44

11. The procedure to follow in the lubrication of maintenance shop equipment is to lubricate 11.____

    A. when you can spare the time
    B. only when necessary
    C. at regular intervals
    D. when the equipment is in operation

12. Of the following items, the one which is NOT used in making fastenings to masonry or plaster walls is a(n) 12.____

    A. lead shield   B. expansion bolt
    C. rawl plug   D. steel bushing

13. When a common straight ladder is used to paint a wall, the safe distance that the foot of the ladder should be set away from the wall is MOST NEARLY _____ the length of the ladder. 13.____

    A. one-eighth   B. one-quarter
    C. one-half   D. five-eighths

14. The term *bell and spigot* usually refers to 14.____

    A. refrigerator motors   B. cast iron pipes
    C. steam radiator outlets D. electrical receptacles

15. In plumbing work, a valve which allows water to flow in one direction only is commonly known as a _____ valve. 15.____

    A. check   B. globe   C. gate   D. stop

16. A pipe coupling is BEST used to connect two pieces of pipe of 16.____

    A. the same diameter in a straight line
    B. the same diameter at right angles to each other
    C. different diameters at a 45° angle
    D. different diameters at an 1/8th bend

17. A fitting or pipe with many outlets relatively close together is commonly called a 17.____

    A. manifold   B. gooseneck
    C. flange union   D. return bend

18. To locate the center in the end of a sound shaft, the BEST tool to use is a(n) 18.____

    A. ruler   B. divider
    C. hermaphrodite caliper   D. micrometer

19. When cutting a piece of 1 1/4" O.D. 20 gauge brass tubing with a hand hacksaw, it is BEST to use a blade having _____ teeth per inch. 19.____

    A. 14   B. 18   C. 22   D. 32

20. When cutting a piece of 1" O.D. extra-heavy pipe with a pipe cutter, a burr usually forms on the inside and the outside of the pipe. These burrs are BEST removed by means of a pipe 20.____

    A. tap and a file   B. wrench and rough stone
    C. reamer and a file   D. drill and a chisel

21. Artificial respiration should be started immediately on a man who has suffered an electric shock if he is

    A. *unconscious* and breathing
    B. *unconscious* and not breathing
    C. *conscious* and in a daze
    D. *conscious* and badly burned

22. The fuse of a certain circuit has blown and is replaced with a fuse of the same rating which also blows when the switch is closed.
    In this case,

    A. a fuse of higher current rating should be used
    B. a fuse of higher voltage rating should be used
    C. the fuse should be temporarily replaced by a heavy piece of wire
    D. the circuit should be checked

23. Operating an incandescent electric light bulb at less than its rated voltage will result in

    A. shorter life and brighter light
    B. longer life and dimmer light
    C. brighter light and longer life
    D. dimmer light and shorter life

24. In order to control a lamp from two different positions, it is necessary to use

    A. two single pole switches
    B. one single pole switch and one four-way switch
    C. two three-way switches
    D. one single pole switch and one four-way switch

25.

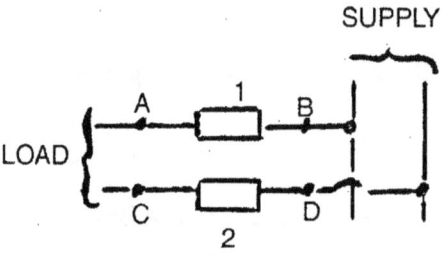

One method of testing fuses is to connect a pair of test lamps in the circuit in such a manner that the test lamp will light up if the fuse is good and will remain dark if the fuse is bad. In the above illustration 1 and 2 are fuses.
In order to test if fuse 1 is bad, test lamps should be connected between

   A. A and B   B. B and D   C. A and D   D. C and B

26. The PRINCIPAL reason for the grounding of electrical equipment and circuits is to

    A. prevent short circuits   B. insure safety from shock
    C. save power   D. increase voltage

27. The ordinary single-pole flush wall type switch must be connected

    A. across the line
    B. in the *hot* conductor
    C. in the grounded conductor
    D. in the white conductor

28. A D.C. shunt motor runs in the wrong direction. This fault can be CORRECTED by

    A. reversing the connections of both the field and the armature
    B. interchanging the connections of either main or auxiliar windings
    C. interchanging the connections to either the field or the armature windings
    D. interchanging the connections to the line of the power leads

29. The MOST common type of motor that can be used with both A.C. and D.C. sources is the _____ motor.

    A. compound   B. repulsion   C. series   D. shunt

30. A fluorescent fixture in a new building has been in use for several months without trouble. Recently, the ends of the fluorscent lamp have remained lighted when the light was switched off.
    The BEST way to clear up this trouble is to replace the

    A. lamp   B. ballast   C. starter   D. sockets

31. The BEST wood to use for handles of tools such as axes and hammers is

    A. hemlock   B. pine   C. oak   D. hickory

32. A *hanger bolt*

    A. has a square head
    B. is bent in a *U* shape
    C. has a different type of thread at each end
    D. is threaded the entire length from point to head

33. A stone frequently used to sharpen tools is

    A. carborundum   B. bauxite   C. resin   D. slate

34. A strike plate is MOST closely associated with a

    A. lock   B. sash   C. butt   D. tie rod

35. The material that distinguishes a terrazzo floor from an ordinary concrete floor is

    A. cinders
    B. marble chip
    C. cut stone
    D. non-slip aggregate

36. A room is 7'6" wide by 9'0" long with a ceiling height of 8'0". One gallon of flat paint will cover approximately 400 square feet of wall.
    The number of gallons of this paint required to paint the walls of this room, making no deductions for windows or doors, is MOST NEARLY _____ gallon.

    A. 1/4   B. 1/2   C. 3/4   D. 1

37. The cost of a certain job is broken down as follows:
    Materials $375
    Rental of equipment 120
    Labor   315
    The percentage of the total cost of the job that can be charged to materials is MOST NEARLY

    A. 40% B. 42% C. 44% D. 46%

38. By trial, it is found that by using two cubic feet of sand, a five cubic foot batch of concrete is produced.
    Using the same proportions, the amount of sand required to produce 2 cubic yards of concrete is MOST NEARLY _____ cu.ft.

    A. 20 B. 22 C. 24 D. 26

39. It takes 4 men 6 days to do a certain job.
    Working at the same speed, the number of days it will take 3 men to do this job is

    A. 7 B. 8 C. 9 D. 10

40. The cost of rawl plugs is $2.75 per gross. The cost of 2,448 rawl plugs is

    A. $46.75 B. $47.25 C. $47.75 D. $48.25

41. *Rigidity of the hammer handle enables the operator to control and direct the force of the blow.*
    As used above, *rigidity* means MOST NEARLY

    A. straightness B. strength
    C. shape   D. stiffness

42. *For precision work, center punches are ground to a fine tapered point.* As used above, *tapered* means MOST NEARLY

    A. conical B. straight C. accurate D. smooth

43. *There are limitations to the drilling of metals by hand power.*
    As used above, *limitations* means MOST NEARLY

    A. advantages   B. restrictions
    C. difficulties D. benefits

Questions 44-45.

DIRECTIONS: Questions 44 and 45 are based on the following paragraph.

Because electric drills run at high speed, the cutting edges of a twist drill are heated quickly. If the metal is thick, the drill point must be withdrawn from the hole frequently to cool it and clear out chips. Forcing the drill continuously into a deep hole will heat it, thereby spoiling its temper and cutting edges. A portable electric drill has the advantage that it can be taken to the work and used to drill holes in material too large to handle in a drill press.

44. According to the above paragraph, overheating of a twist drill will

    A. slow down the work B. cause excessive drill breakage
    C. dull the drill   D. spoil the accuracy of the work

45. According to the above paragraph, one method of preventing overheating of a twist drill is to   45.____

    A. use cooling oil
    B. drill a smaller pilot hole first
    C. use a drill press
    D. remove the drill from the work frequently

Questions 46-50.

DIRECTIONS: Questions 46 to 50 are to be answered in accordance with the sketch shown below.

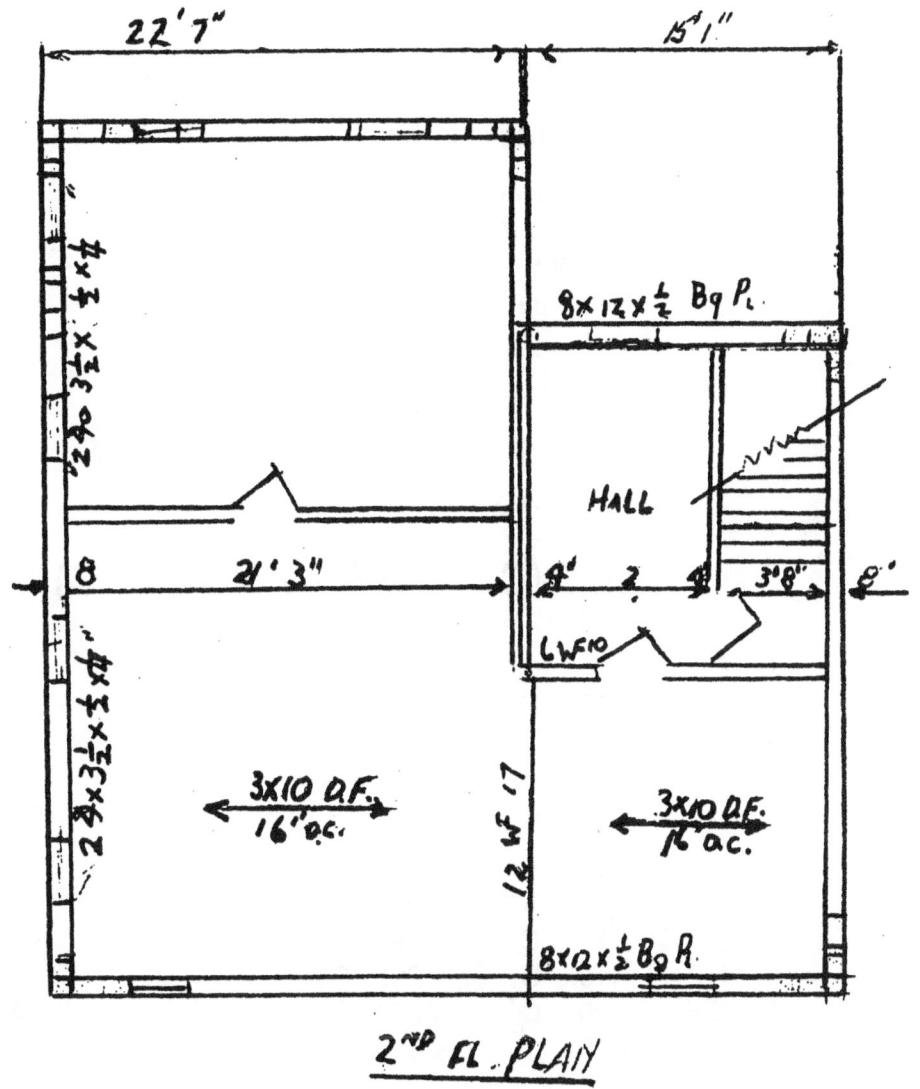

2ND FL. PLAN

46. The one of the following statements that is CORRECT is the building   46.____

    A. is of fireproof construction
    B. has masonry walls with wood joists
    C. is of wood frame construction
    D. has timber joists and girders

47. The one of the following statements that is CORRECT is 47.____

    A. the stairway from the ground continues through the roof
    B. there are two means of egress from the second floor of this building
    C. the door on the second floor stair landing opens in the direction of egress
    D. the entire stair is shown on this plan

48. The width of the hall is 48.____

    A. 10'3"   B. 10'5"   C. 10'7"   D. 10'9"

49. The lintels shown are 49.____

    A. angles
    C. an I-beam
    B. a channel and an angle
    D. precast concrete

50. The one of the following statements that is CORRECT is that the steel beam is 50.____

    A. supported by columns at the center and at the ends
    B. entirely supported by the walls
    C. supported on columns at the ends only
    D. supported at the center by a column and at the ends by the walls

---

KEY (CORRECT ANSWERS)

1. B	11. C	21. B	31. D	41. D
2. B	12. D	22. D	32. C	42. A
3. A	13. B	23. B	33. A	43. B
4. B	14. B	24. C	34. A	44. C
5. C	15. A	25. C	35. B	45. D
6. C	16. A	26. B	36. C	46. B
7. B	17. A	27. B	37. D	47. C
8. D	18. C	28. C	38. B	48. D
9. B	19. D	29. C	39. B	49. A
10. D	20. C	30. C	40. A	50. D

EXAMINATION SECTION
TEST 1

DIRECTIONS: Each question consists of a statement. You are to indicate whether the statement is TRUE (T) or FALSE (F). *PRINT THE LETTER OF THE CORRECT ANSWER IN THE SPACE AT THE RIGHT.*

1. One square foot is equal to 144 square inches.   1.____

2. One cubic foot of water weighs APPROXIMATELY 8 1/2 pounds.   2.____

3. One bag of portland cement weighs APPROXIMATELY 94 pounds.   3.____

4. If a board foot is 12 inches by 12 inches by one inch, the number of board feet in a plank 18 feet long, 10 inches wide, 4 inches thick is 360.   4.____

5. If a cubic foot of water contains 7 1/2 gallons, the number of gallons contained in a tank 6 feet long, 4 feet wide, and 2 feet deep is 360.   5.____

6. The total surface area of a 6 inch solid cube is 144 square inches.   6.____

7. 1728 cubic feet equal 192 cubic yards.   7.____

8. When the mix proportion for a concrete sidewalk is given as 1:3:5, the numbers give the ratio by volume of cement to sand to coarse aggregate.   8.____

9. When oily waste rags are not in use, it is good practice to store them in self-closing metal containers.   9.____

10. The CHIEF purpose of a trap under a plumbing fixture is to act as a seal against sewer gas.   10.____

11. If a rectangular frame measures 12 inches long and 9 inches wide, the length of its diagonal is 21 inches.   11.____

12. Threads on the inside of metal pipes are usually cut with dies.   12.____

13. A screwdriver is the proper tool to drive a lag screw into place.   13.____

14. The diameter of one inch pipe is measured from the outside of the pipe.   14.____

15. If the counterweights of the top sash of a window are too heavy, more exertion will be necessary to close that half of the window.   15.____

16. Glazed tile should be wet prior to being laid.   16.____

17. The striking plate is part of a lockset.   17.____

18. A casement window usually slides up and down.   18.____

19. An escutcheon plate is part of a lockset.   19.____

20. When using a hand saw, it is good practice to pull up rather than push down the saw when starting the first stroke.   20.____

21. Hickory is a very brittle wood. 21.____

22. Timber which is continually wet will not rot as soon as timber which is alternately wet and dry. 22.____

23. A nosing is the projecting edge of a stair tread. 23.____

24. When sawing wood marked off with a pencil line, the saw should be driven through the center of the pencil line. 24.____

25. One 45 degree elbow fitting will make a right angle. 25.____

26. The MOST probable cause of the water of a flush tank of a toilet continuing to flow after the flushing has stopped is that the rubber ball fails to seat properly. 26.____

27. Nails driven with the grain of the wood do not hold as well as when driven across the grain. 27.____

28. Usually sandpapering of wood should be done with the grain. 28.____

29. After concrete sidewalks are poured in the open air, they are usually covered with straw or paper in order to give a bright color to the sidewalk. 29.____

30. To prevent screws from splitting the wood when they are being driven, it is good practice to drill a small hole first. 30.____

31. The PRINCIPAL purpose of a leader is to carry away sewage from a building. 31.____

32. The PRINCIPAL purpose of a hacksaw is to cut thin wood. 32.____

33. The board around a room at the bottom of the walls is known as a baseboard. 33.____

34. Clay tiles, when used on the interior of buildings, are usually set in Portland cement mortar. 34.____

35. Before window glass is set in wooden window sashes, putty should be placed in the rebates of the sash. 35.____

36. Clear window glass is made in ONLY one thickness. 36.____

37. Glass which is to be set in wooden sash windows should be cut to the exact measurements between the sashes. 37.____

38. Three eighths (3/8") of an inch is equivalent to .0375". 38.____

39. Nipples are short pieces of pipe threaded only on one end. 39.____

40. Pipe fittings which connect pipes so that they may be at an angle to each other are known as elbows. 40.____

41. Solder is a mixture of lead and brass. 41.____

42. A yellow flame in the burner of a gas range usually indicates that the proper amount of air for combustion is present. 42.____

43. Gaskets are generally used to relieve clogged drain pipes. 43.____

44. The PRINCIPAL purpose of galvanizing iron is to prevent rust. 44.____

45. When driving a long nail into a piece of wood, it is good practice to start hammering with light blows. 45.____

46. If a maintenance man is to remove a door having two hinges from its frame, he should FIRST remove the lower hinge. 46.____

47. If a 10 ampere fuse blows out constantly, it should be replaced with a 15 ampere fuse. 47.____

48. When grinding a tool, the stone should revolve towards the bevel edge of the tool that is pressed against it. 48.____

49. The upright members of a wooden door are known as rails. 49.____

50. Casement windows are balanced with weights. 50.____

KEY (CORRECT ANSWERS)

1.	T	11.	F	21.	F	31.	F	41.	F
2.	F	12.	F	22.	T	32.	F	42.	F
3.	T	13.	F	23.	T	33.	T	43.	F
4.	F	14.	F	24.	F	34.	T	44.	T
5.	T	15.	F	25.	F	35.	T	45.	T
6.	F	16.	T	26.	T	36.	F	46.	T
7.	F	17.	T	27.	T	37.	F	47.	F
8.	T	18.	F	28.	T	38.	F	48.	T
9.	T	19.	T	29.	F	39.	F	49.	F
10.	T	20.	T	30.	T	40.	T	50.	F

TEST 2

DIRECTIONS: Each question consists of a statement. You are to indicate whether the statement is TRUE (T) or FALSE (F). *PRINT THE LETTER OF THE CORRECT ANSWER IN THE SPACE AT THE RIGHT.*

1. Stillson wrench is another name for a monkey wrench. 1.____

2. To draw a nail from a board with a claw hammer, the greatest drawing power will result when the handle of the hammer is held at the end farthest from the head. 2.____

3. To remove paint spots from a wooden desk, it is BETTER to use turpentine rather than linseed oil. 3.____

4. The water level in the flushing tank of a water closet should not be lower than the overflow opening, 4.____

5. The BEST method of repairing cracks in a toilet bowl of solid porcelain is to putty them. 5.____

6. When making concrete by hand, the sand and cement should be nixed together before adding water. 6.____

7. To lift a heavy object from the floor, a person should keep the legs straight and do the lifting with his back. 7.____

8. It is not good practice to report accidents on a job when they do not seem to be serious. 8.____

9. Tools used by workmen should generally be cleaned before storing away each night. 9.____

10. If a maintenance man receives an order from his foreman to do a job which he does not understand, he should use his own judgment and go ahead with the job. 10.____

11. The legs of a compass should be spread 5 inches apart in order to draw a circle with a diameter 5 inches. 11.____

12. A box measuring 18 inches square and 16 inches deep will have a volume of 36 cubic feet. 12.____

13. When setting glass in windows, it is good practice to give the wood a coat of linseed oil before applying the putty. 13.____

14. A nail set is used to drive wood screws beneath the surface of the floor. 14.____

15. When replacing a door in its frame, the top hinge should be attached before the bottom hinge. 15.____

16. A ripsaw is the proper tool for cutting metal pipe. 16.____

17. In cold weather the temperature of a room may be lowered due to conduction of heat through window glass. 17.____

18. The object of marking off sidewalks into rectangular slabs is to prevent pedestrians slipping on the completed walk. 18.____

19. The CHIEF purpose in keeping tools and supplies in orderly manner is to discourage theft of the tools.   19.____

20. The horizontal members of a wooden door are known as rails.   20.____

21. A wood chisel is sharpened only on one side.   21.____

22. A screwdriver is the proper tool for driving a nail below the surface of the wood.   22.____

23. Putty for window glazing is usually made of cement and linseed oil.   23.____

24. Hickory is a suitable wood for handles of hammers.   24.____

25. The number on the saw blade of a carpenter's saw near the handle indicates the width of the saw at the point.   25.____

26. The vertical part of stair steps is called the riser.   26.____

27. A reamer is the CORRECT tool with which to put threads on a pipe.   27.____

28. A person should face the ladder as he descends on it.   28.____

29. A center punch is used for marking points on metal at which holes are to be drilled.   29.____

30. A stud bolt has a square head.   30.____

31. The teeth of saws are usually bent sideways alternately to prevent saw binding in the cut slot.   31.____

32. When inserting a pane of window glass in a wooden window sash, glazier's points should be forced into the sash after the puttying has been completed.   32.____

33. Lead poisoning may result after eating meals while red lead or lead filings are under the nails of the hands of the worker.   33.____

34. A coupling is a pipe fitting with internal threads.   34.____

35. A tee joint for pipe has 3 openings.   35.____

36. A die is generally used to cut threads in a nut.   36.____

37. Glass is a good electrical conductor.   37.____

38. Small nails used in fine work are called rivets.   38.____

39. A fuse wire should melt less readily than the wiring in the circuit which it protects.   39.____

40. The diameter of a circle is equal to half its circumference.   40.____

41. The unit of electrical resistance is the ampere.   41.____

42. Where only a short swing of the handle is possible, the ratchet type wrench is best used.   42.____

43. Iron coated with tin is called galvanized iron.   43.____

44. An advantage of cast iron is that it bends very easily but does not break.   44.____

45. Monel metal rusts very quickly.

46. A *compass* saw is best used for cutting heavy boards.

47. Brads are used to fasten heavy boards together.

48. When used in connection with nails, *penny* refers to quality.

49. An expansion bolt is usually used to allow for expansion and contraction due to climatic conditions.

50. The French polish finish is the FINEST shellac finish that there is.

KEY (CORRECT ANSWERS)

1. F	11. F	21. T	31. T	41. F
2. T	12. F	22. F	32. F	42. T
3. T	13. T	23. F	33. T	43. F
4. F	14. F	24. T	34. T	44. F
5. F	15. T	25. F	35. T	45. F
6. T	16. F	26. T	36. F	46. F
7. F	17. T	27. F	37. T	47. F
8. F	18. F	28. T	38. F	48. F
9. T	19. F	29. T	39. F	49. F
10. F	20. T	30. F	40. F	50. T

TEST 3

DIRECTIONS: Each question consists of a statement. You are to indicate whether the statement is TRUE (T) or FALSE (F). *PRINT THE LETTER OF THE CORRECT ANSWER IN THE SPACE AT THE RIGHT.*

1. To lay out very precise work on wood, it is BEST to use a chalk line.   1.____

2. A ripsaw is BEST used for cutting wood across the grain.   2.____

3. Beach sand, because of its uniform grain, will make a dense and strong concrete.   3.____

4. A *union* is the same as a *coupling* in plumbing.   4.____

5. A valve that permits free passage of water through a pipe or valve in one direction, but prevents a reversal of flow, is called a check valve.   5.____

6. Iron or steel fittings used with brass or copper pipe would cause an electrical action that would be unsatisfactory.   6.____

7. Brass and copper are USUALLY softer than iron or steel.   7.____

8. While pipe is being cut to length and threaded, it is held securely in place usually by a pipe vise.   8.____

9. With respect to water closets, pressure flush valves are usually used without a tank.   9.____

10. Troubles resulting from low velocity of liquids flowing through horizontal pipes are greatly lessened by giving these pipes a downward pitch toward the soil.   10.____

11. Water is delivered to the building under pressure from a street main. The pipe coming into the building is usually called the downtake pipe.   11.____

12. Elbows usually have female threads at both ends.   12.____

13. Extensive tests have shown that the strength of timber is increased as its moisture content is decreased.   13.____

14. Thawing a frozen water pipe by means of a blowtorch is highly recommended.   14.____

15. Heat applied to a frozen water pipe should be applied first at the middle of the frozen part.   15.____

16. Water closet traps may be cleaned with a tool called a closet auger. This is usually operated by compressed air.   16.____

17. With respect to faucet washers, leather and fibre washers are satisfactory for cold water, but composition materials generally last longer on the hot water side.   17.____

18. A pipe cutter leaves a larger burr on the outside of a pipe than on the inside.   18.____

19. In threading pipe, dirt and chips in the stock and die will result in imperfect threads.   19.____

20. The burr resulting from cutting pipe is BEST removed by a pipe tapper.   20.____

21. With respect to pipe, the abbreviation I.P.S. means iron pipe shape. 21.____

22. Caustic potash when used as a drain pipe solvent will NOT damage aluminum. 22.____

23. Any pipe which carries the discharge from one or more water closets to the house drain is called a soil pipe. 23.____

24. A vent stack is a vertical pipe whose primary purpose is to allow circulation of air to and from any other piping in the drainage system of the building. 24.____

25. Evaporation may gradually reduce the depth of trap water in case a fixture remains unused for long periods. 25.____

26. The rubber ball stopper in a flush tank is held in place normally by air pressure. 26.____

27. In water closets an overflow tube allows water to flow into the closet bowl should the ball cock fail to close and the level rises too high in the tank. 27.____

28. When the ground seat in a compression faucet has become pitted or grooved, the seat should be dressed down true with a reamer. 28.____

29. A chamfer is a kind of bevel. 29.____

30. A corrugated fastener for joining two pieces of wood can sometimes be used in place of a nail.
It should be driven by heavy blows from a heavy hammer. 30.____

31. No. 1 sandpaper is finer than number 4 sandpaper. 31.____

32. To *rod* a sewer pipe means to support the sewer pipe with reinforcing metal rods. 32.____

33. *T* and *G*, when applied to lumber, means tested and guaranteed. 33.____

34. When a screwdriver is used on a small object, the object should be held in the palm of the hand. 34.____

35. An oval faced hammer is BEST for driving nails. 35.____

36. Metal sash chains are usually of the flat link type. 36.____

37. A casement window can swing only one way, and that way is out. 37.____

38. The mark *UL* on electrical equipment usually means universal license. 38.____

39. Every door closing or checking device must be mounted overhead on the door. 39.____

40. A wash basin with a pop up drain always has a stopper and chain. 40.____

41. A fusible plug is usually used to make a temporary repair on a leaking water pipe. 41.____

42. To be effective, a thermostat must always have a clock connected with it. 42.____

43. Wood with narrow annual rings is denser and stronger than wood with wide annual rings. 43.____

44. BX in the electrical industry means best grade. 44.____

45. A sub-metering device means a device usually buried and underground in the street. 45.____
46. An oscillating fan is designed to run faster automatically as the room temperature rises. 46.____
47. An electrical cooking stove requires a *booster* to light a burner. 47.____
48. A universal motor is designed to operate with either A.C. or D.C. power. 48.____
49. An A.C. fuse will NOT operate on D.C. 49.____
50. Special circuit wiring is required for the installation of fluorescent lighting fixtures. 50.____

KEY (CORRECT ANSWERS)

1. F	11. F	21. F	31. T	41. F
2. F	12. T	22. F	32. F	42. F
3. F	13. T	23. T	33. F	43. T
4. F	14. F	24. T	34. F	44. F
5. T	15. F	25. T	35. F	45. F
6. T	16. F	26. F	36. T	46. F
7. T	17. T	27. T	37. F	47. F
8. T	18. F	28. F	38. F	48. T
9. T	19. T	29. T	39. F	49. F
10. T	20. F	30. F	40. F	50. F

TEST 4

DIRECTIONS: Each question consists of a statement. You are to indicate whether the statement is TRUE (T) or FALSE (F). *PRINT THE LETTER OF THE CORRECT ANSWER IN THE SPACE AT THE RIGHT.*

1. *Scotch* tape is preferable to friction tape for the splicing of electrical conductors.   1.____
2. With respect to passenger elevators, car doors and shaft doors are the same.   2.____
3. A pendant fixture is a fixture hanging or suspended.   3.____
4. A rectifier changes A.C. to D.C. current.   4.____
5. A knife switch is used to cut small sections of wire from a spool of wire.   5.____
6. Domestic electric bills are usually rendered for kilowatt hours consumed.   6.____
7. When lamps are connected in series, if one goes out, all go out.   7.____
8. A household iron usually consumes about 110 watts.   8.____
9. The dry cell battery supplies alternating current.   9.____
10. On the dry cell battery, one terminal is called the positive and the other is called the negative.   10.____
11. An annunciator is a device to change the voltage of a current of electricity.   11.____
12. The average household electric bulb contains air under heavy pressure.   12.____
13. Insulators offer high resistance to the flow of electricity.   13.____
14. The smaller the wire, the larger the current carrying capacity of the wire.   14.____
15. #14 wire is smaller than #8 wire.   15.____
16. Transformers can operate only on A.C.   16.____
17. Some cartridge fuses are renewable by replacing the fuse element.   17.____
18. A *short* in a circuit should *blow* the fuse.   18.____
19. A circuit breaker is a type of conduit.   19.____
20. A miter box is used to store small nails, washers, and tools on the job.   20.____
21. When a hidden edge is shown on a drawing, it is represented by a dotted line.   21.____
22. A rasp is a kind of heavy hammer.   22.____
23. *Green* lumber is lumber not well seasoned.   23.____
24. A dowel is usually triangular in shape.   24.____
25. Monkey wrenches usually have jaws with teeth.   25.____

2 (#4)

26. The only material that can cut glass is a diamond, or diamond chip. 26.____
27. An extension ladder and a step ladder are the same. 27.____
28. A turnbuckle is a type of general purpose wrench. 28.____
29. Terrazzo is a kind of concealed joint used in expensive cabinet work. 29.____
30. A burr is a kind of metal measuring tape. 30.____
31. Armored cable is cable with a soft outer covering but with very heavy inside wire. 31.____
32. Continued use of a portable electric room heater will *use up* the oxygen in a small closed room quicker than a gas heater. 32.____
33. Plate glass is generally superior to sheet glass for windows. 33.____
34. White pine is a harder wood than white oak. 34.____
35. Chestnut is usually considered an *open grained* wood. 35.____
36. #30 sheet iron is thicker than #14. 36.____
37. Semi-vitreous tiles are generally harder than vitreous tiles. 37.____
38. One disadvantage of interlocking rubber tiling is that it is *noisy* in use. 38.____
39. A *light* of glass is the same as a *pane* of glass. 39.____
40. The scratch coat of plaster is the last coat to be applied. 40.____
41. The riser pipe in a heating system is usually horizontal. 41.____
42. With reference to wire specifications, AWG means American Wire Gage. 42.____
43. Electric motors are never rated in terms of horsepower. 43.____
44. The use of self-closing water faucets should help reduce water waste. 44.____
45. *Push button* elevators are manufactured only by the Otis Elevator Company. 45.____
46. Gas bills are usually computed on the basis of cubic feet consumed. 46.____
47. With respect to pipe, I.D. usually means inside diameter. 47.____
48. Graphite is sometimes used as a lubricant. 48.____
49. A blow torch can burn gasoline only. 49.____
50. Bronze is composed CHIEFLY of copper and tin. 50.____

KEY (CORRECT ANSWERS)

1. F	11. F	21. T	31. F	41. F
2. F	12. F	22. F	32. F	42. T
3. T	13. T	23. T	33. T	43. F
4. T	14. F	24. F	34. F	44. T
5. F	15. T	25. F	35. T	45. F
6. T	16. T	26. F	36. F	46. T
7. T	17. T	27. F	37. F	47. T
8. F	18. T	28. F	38. F	48. T
9. F	19. F	29. F	39. T	49. F
10. T	20. F	30. F	40. F	50. T

———

EXAMINATION SECTION
TEST 1

DIRECTIONS: Each question or incomplete statement is followed by several suggested answers or completions. Select the one that BEST answers the question or completes the statement. *PRINT THE LETTER OF THE CORRECT ANSWER IN THE SPACE AT THE RIGHT.*

1. A bit is held in a hand drill by means of a(n) 1._____
    A. arbor B. chuck C. collet D. clamp

2. The type of screw that MOST often requires a countersunk hole is a _____ head. 2._____
    A. flat B. round C. fillister D. hexagon

3. Instead of using the ordinary 1 piece screwdriver, a screwdriver bit is MOST often used with a brace because of the 3._____
    A. increased length of the brace
    B. different types of bits available
    C. increased leverage of the brace
    D. ability to work in tight corners

4. A thread gage is usually used to measure the 4._____
    A. thickness of a thread
    B. diameter of a thread
    C. number of threads per inch
    D. height of a thread

5. The wheel of a glass cutter is BEST lubricated with 5._____
    A. kerosene
    B. linseed oil
    C. varnolene
    D. diesel oil

6. A nail set is a 6._____
    A. group of nails of the same size and type
    B. group of nails of different sizes but the same type
    C. tool used to extract nails
    D. tool used to drive nails below the surface of wood

7. To test for leaks in a gas line, it is BEST to use 7._____
    A. a match
    B. soapy water
    C. a colored dye
    D. ammonia

8. Routing is the process of cutting a 8._____
    A. strip out of sheet metal
    B. groove in wood
    C. chamfer on a shaft
    D. core out of concrete

9. A hacksaw frame has a wing nut mainly to 9._____
    A. make it easier to replace blades
    B. increase the strength of the frame
    C. prevent vibration of the blade
    D. adjust the length of the frame

10. A mitre box is usually used with a _____ saw.

    A. hack   B. crosscut   C. rip   D. back

11. A continuous flexible saw blade is MOST often used on a _____ saw.

    A. radial   B. band   C. swing   D. table

12. A pipe reamer is used to

    A. clean out a length of pipe
    B. thread pipe
    C. remove burrs from the ends of pipe
    D. seal pipe joints

13. To lay out a straight cut on a piece of wood at the same angle as the cut on a second piece of wood, the PROPER tool to use is a

    A. bevel   B. cope   C. butt gauge   D. clevis

14. Before drilling a hole in a piece of metal, an indentation should be made with a _____ punch.

    A. pin   B. taper   C. center   D. drift

15. Curved cuts in wood are BEST made with a _____ saw.

    A. jig   B. veneer   C. radial   D. swing

16. A face plate is generally used to

    A. hold material while working with it on a lathe
    B. smooth out irregularities in a metal plate
    C. protect the finish on a metal plate
    D. locate centers of holes to be drilled on a drill press

17. A die would be used to

    A. gage the groove in a splined shaft
    B. cut a thread on a metal rod
    C. hold a piece to be machined on a milling machine
    D. control the depth of a hole to be drilled in a piece of metal

18. Before using a ladle to scoop up molten solder, you should make sure that the ladle is dry.
    This is done to prevent

    A. the solder from sticking to the ladle
    B. impurities from getting into the solder
    C. injuries due to splashing solder
    D. cooling of the solder

19. To PROPERLY adjust the gap on a spark plug, you should use a(n) 19._____
    A. inside caliper   B. center gauge
    C. wire type feeler gauge D. micrometer

20. The length of the MOST common type of folding wood rule is _____ feet. 20._____
    A. 4   B. 5   C. 6   D. 7

21. A four-foot mason's level is usually used to determine whether the top of a wall is level and whether it is 21._____
    A. square   B. plumb   C. rigid   D. in line

22. To match a tongue in a board, the matching board MUST have a 22._____
    A. rabbet   B. chamfer   C. bead   D. groove

23. When driving screws in close quarters, the BEST type of screwdriver to use is a(n) 23._____
    A. Phillips   B. offset   C. butt   D. angled

24. The term 12-24 refers to a _____ screw. 24._____
    A. wood   B. lag
    C. sheet metal   D. machine

25. To measure the length of a curved line on a drawing or plan, the PROPER tool to use in addition to a ruler is(are) 25._____
    A. dividers   B. calipers
    C. surface gage D. radius gage

26. For the standard machine screw, the diameter of a tap drill is generally 26._____
    A. *equal* to the diameter of the shaft of the screw at the base of the threads (the root diameter)
    B. *larger* than the root diameter, but smaller than the diameter of the screw
    C. *equal* to the diameter of the screw
    D. *larger* than the diameter of the screw

27. In order to drill a 1" hole accurately with a drill press, you should 27._____
    A. drill at high speeds
    B. use very little pressure on the drill
    C. drill partway down, release pressure on the drill, and then continue drilling
    D. drill a pilot hole first

28. Before taking apart an electric motor to repair, punch marks are sometimes placed on the casing near each other.
    The MOST probable reason for doing this is to 28._____
    A. make sure the parts lock together on reassembly
    B. properly line up the parts that are next to each other
    C. keep track of the number of parts in the assembly
    D. identify all the parts as coming from the one motor

29. To locate a point on a floor directly under a point on the ceiling, the PROPER tool to use is a   29._____

    A. square B. line level
    C. height gage D. plumb bob

Question 30.

DIRECTIONS: Question 30 is based on the diagram appearing below.

30. In the above diagram, the full P required to lift the weight a distance of four feet is MOST NEARLY _____ lbs.   30._____

    A. 50 B. 67 C. 75 D. 100

31. The EASIEST tool to use to determine whether the edge of a board is at right angles to the face of the board is a   31._____

    A. rafter square B. try square
    C. protractor D. marking gage

32. *Whetting* refers to   32._____

    A. tempering of tools by dipping them in water
    B. annealing of tools by heating and slow cooling
    C. brazing of carbide tips on tools
    D. sharpening of tools

33. The MOST difficult part of a plank to plane is the   33._____

    A. face B. side C. end D. back

34. To prevent wood from splitting when drilling with an auger, it is BEST to   34._____

    A. use even pressure on the bit
    B. drill at a slow speed
    C. hold the wood tightly in a vise
    D. back up the wood with a piece of scrap wood

35. The term *dressing a grinding wheel* refers to 35.____

    A. setting up the wheel on the arbor
    B. restoring the sharpness of a wheel face that has become clogged
    C. placing flanges against the sides of the wheel
    D. bringing the wheel up to speed before using it

36. Heads of rivets are BEST cut off with a 36.____

    A. hacksaw   B. cold chisel
    C. fly cutter   D. reamer

37. A *V-block* is especially useful to 37.____

    A. prevent damage to work held in a vise
    B. hold round stock while a hole is being drilled into it
    C. prevent rolling of round stock stored on the ground
    D. shim up the end of a machine so that it is level

38. A full set of taps for a given size usually consists of a _____ tap. 38.____

    A. taper and bottoming
    B. taper and plug
    C. plug and bottoming
    D. taper, plug, and bottoming

39. Round thread cutting dies are usually held in stock by means of 39.____

    A. wing nuts   B. clamps   C. set screws   D. bolts

40. The one of the following diagrams that shows the plan view and the elevation of a counterbored hole is 40.____

A.

B.

C.

D.

41. With regard to pipe, *I.D.* usually means 41.____

    A. inside diameter   B. inside dressed
    C. invert diameter   D. installation date

42. A compression fitting is MOST often used to

    A. lubricate a wheel
    B. join two pieces of tubing
    C. reduce the diameter of a hole
    D. press fit a gear to a shaft

43. The shape of a mill file is basically

    A. flat   B. half round   C. triangular   D. square

44. Of the following, the ratio of tin to lead that will produce the solder with the LOWEST melting point is

    A. 30-70   B. 40-60   C. 50-50   D. 60-40

45. A safe edge on a file is one that

    A. is smooth and can not cut
    B. has a finer cut than the face of the file
    C. is rounded to prevent scratches
    D. has a coarser cut than the face of the file

46. The MOST frequent use of a file card is to _____ files.

    A. sort out   B. clean
    C. prevent damage to   D. prevent clogging of

47. The BEST way of determining whether a grinding wheel has an internal crack is to

    A. run the wheel at high speed, stop it, and examine the wheel
    B. spray lubricating oil on the sides of the wheel and check the amount of absorption of the oil
    C. hit the wheel with a rubber hammer and listen to the sound
    D. drop the wheel sharply on a table and then check the wheel

48. If a grinding wheel has worn to a smaller diameter, the BEST practice to follow is to

    A. discard the wheel
    B. continue using the wheel as before
    C. use the wheel, but at a faster speed
    D. use the wheel, but at a slower speed

49. With respect to the ordinary awl,

    A. only the tip is hardened
    B. the entire blade is hardened
    C. the tip is tempered, and the rest of the blade is hardened
    D. the entire blade is tempered

50. To prevent overheating of drills, it is BEST to use _____ oil.

    A. cutting   B. lubricating
    C. penetrating   D. heating

KEY (CORRECT ANSWERS)

1. B	11. B	21. B	31. B	41. A
2. A	12. C	22. D	32. D	42. B
3. C	13. A	23. B	33. C	43. A
4. C	14. C	24. D	34. D	44. D
5. A	15. A	25. A	35. B	45. A
6. D	16. A	26. B	36. B	46. B
7. B	17. B	27. D	37. B	47. C
8. B	18. C	28. B	38. D	48. C
9. A	19. C	29. D	39. C	49. A
10. D	20. C	30. D	40. A	50. A

TEST 2

DIRECTIONS: Each question or incomplete statement is followed by several suggested answers or completions. Select the one that BEST answers the question or completes the statement. *PRINT THE LETTER OF THE CORRECT ANSWER IN THE SPACE AT THE RIGHT.*

1. Crocus cloth is commonly used to   1.____

    A. protect finely machined surfaces from damage while the machines are being repaired
    B. remove rust from steel
    C. protect floors and furniture while painting walls
    D. wipe up oil and grease that has spilled

2. Before using a new paint brush, the FIRST operation should be to   2.____

    A. remove loose bristles
    B. soak the brush in linseed oil
    C. hang the brush up overnight
    D. clean the brush with turpentine

3. When sharpening a hand saw, the FIRST operation is to   3.____

    A. file the teeth down to the same height
    B. shape the teeth to the proper profile
    C. bend the teeth over to provide clearance when sawing
    D. clean the gullies with a file

4. To prevent solder from dripping when soldering a vertical seam, it is BEST to   4.____

    A. hold a waxed rag under the soldering iron
    B. use the soldering iron in a horizontal position
    C. tin the soldering iron on one side only
    D. solder the seam in the order from bottom to top

5. If a round nut has two holes in the face, the PROPER type wrench to use to tighten this nut is a(n)   5.____

    A. Stillson   B. monkey   C. spanner   D. open end

6. A box wrench is BEST used on   6.____

    A. pipe fittings   B. flare nuts
    C. hexagonal nuts   D. Allen screws

7. To prevent damage to fine finishes on metal work that is to be held in a vise, you should   7.____

    A. clamp the work lightly
    B. use brass inserts on the vise
    C. wrap the work with cloth before inserting it in the vise
    D. substitute a smooth face plate for the serrated plate on the vise

8. The MOST frequent use for a turnbuckle is to

   A. tighten a guy wire
   B. adjust shims on a machine
   C. bolt a bracket to a wall
   D. support electric cable from a ceiling

9. To form the head of a tinner's rivet, the PROPER tool to use is a rivet

   A. anvil   B. plate   C. set   D. brake

10. A socket speed handle MOST closely resembles a

    A. screwdriver   B. brace   C. spanner   D. spin grip

11. Tips of masonry drills are usually made of

    A. steel   B. carbide   C. corundum   D. monel

12. The BEST flux to use for soldering galvanized iron is

    A. resin
    B. sal ammoniac
    C. borax
    D. muriatic acid

13. The one of the following that is NOT a common type of oilstone is

    A. silicon carbide
    B. aluminum oxide
    C. hard Arkansas
    D. pumice

14. A method of joining metals using temperatures intermediate between soldering and welding is

    A. corbelling   B. brazing   C. annealing   D. lapping

15. When an unusually high degree of accuracy is required with woodwork, lines should be marked with a

    A. pencil ground to a chisel point
    B. pencil line over a crayon line
    C. sharp knife point
    D. scriber

16. The MOST important difference between pipe threads and V threads on bolts is that pipe threads are usually

    A. longer
    B. sharper
    C. tapered
    D. more evenly spaced

17. A street elbow differs from the ordinary elbow in that the street elbow has

    A. different diameter threads at each end
    B. male threads at one end and female threads at the other
    C. female threads at both ends
    D. male threads at both ends

18. Water hammer in a pipe line can MOST often be stopped by the installation of a(n)

    A. pressure reducing valve
    B. expansion joint
    C. flexible coupling
    D. air chamber

19. If water is leaking from the top part of a bibcock, the part that should be replaced is MOST likely the

   A. bibb washer
   B. packing
   C. seat
   D. bibb screw

20. When joining electric wires together in a fixture box, the BEST thing to use are wire

   A. connectors
   B. couplings
   C. clamps
   D. bolts

21. If the name plate of a motor indicates that it is a split phase motor, it is LIKELY that this motor

   A. is a universal motor
   B. operates on DC only
   C. operates on AC only
   D. operates either on DC at full power or on AC at reduced power

22. To make driving of a screw into hard wood easier, it is BEST to lubricate the threads of the screw with

   A. varnoline
   B. penetrating oil
   C. beeswax
   D. cutting oil

23. Assume that a thermostatically controlled oil heater fails to operate. To determine whether it is the thermostat that is at fault, you should

   A. check the circuit breaker
   B. connect a wire across the terminals of the thermostat
   C. replace the contacts on the thermostat
   D. put an ammeter on the line

24. The function of the carburetor on a gasoline engine is to

   A. mix the air and gasoline properly
   B. filter the fuel
   C. filter the air to engine
   D. pump the gasoline into the cylinder

25. If a car owner complains that the battery in his car is constantly running dry, the item that should be checked FIRST is the

   A. fan belt
   B. generator
   C. voltage regulator
   D. relay

26. On MOST modern automobiles, foot brake pressure is transmitted to the brake drums by

   A. air pressure
   B. mechanical linkage
   C. hydraulic fluid
   D. electro-magnetic force

27. Assume that the engine of a car remains cold even though it is run for a period of time. The part that is MOST likely at fault is the

   A. heat by-pass valve
   B. thermostat
   C. heater control
   D. choke

28. To permit easy stripping of concrete forms, they should be

   A. dried   B. oiled   C. wet down   D. cleaned

29. To prevent honey combing in concrete, the concrete should be

   A. vibrated
   B. cured
   C. heated in cold weather
   D. protected from the rain

30. The MAIN reason for using wire mesh in connection with concrete work is to

   A. strain the impurities from the sand
   B. increase the strength of the concrete
   C. hold the forms together
   D. protect the concrete till it hardens

31. Segregation of concrete is MOST often caused by pouring concrete

   A. in cold weather
   B. from too great a height
   C. too rapidly
   D. into a form in which the concrete has already begun to harden

32. Headers in carpentry are MOST closely associated with

   A. trimmers
   B. cantilevers
   C. posts
   D. newels

33. Joists are very often supported by

   A. suspenders
   B. base plates
   C. anchor bolts
   D. bridal irons

34. At outside corners, the type of joint MOST frequently used on a baseboard is the

   A. plowed
   B. mitered
   C. mortise and tenon
   D. butt

35. The vehicle used with latex paints is usually

   A. linseed oil
   B. shellac
   C. varnish
   D. water

36. *Boxing* of paint refers to the _____ of paints.

   A. mixing   B. storage   C. use   D. canning

37. When painting wood, nail holes should be puttied

   A. *before* applying the prime coat
   B. *after* applying the prime coat but before the second coat
   C. *after* applying the second coat but before the third coat
   D. *after* applying the third coat

38. In laying up a brick wall, you find that at the end of the wall there is not enough space for a full brick.
    You should use a

   A. stretcher   B. bat   C. corbel   D. bull nose

39. Pointing a brick wall is the same as 39.____

    A. truing up the wall
    B. topping the wall with a waterproof surface
    C. repairing the mortar joints in the wall
    D. providing a foundation for the wall

40. The pigment MOST often used in a prime coat of paint on steel to prevent rusting is 40.____

    A. lampblack   B. calcimine
    C. zinc oxide   D. red lead

41. If you find a co-worker lying unconscious across an electric wire, the FIRST thing you should do is 41.____

    A. get him off the wire   B. call the foreman
    C. get a doctor   D. shut off the power

42. 42.____

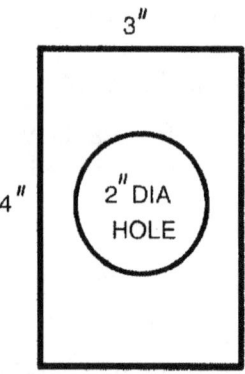

The area of the metal plate shown above, minus the hole area, is MOST NEARLY _____ square inches.

   A. 8.5   B. 8.9   C. 9.4   D. 10.1

43. 43.____

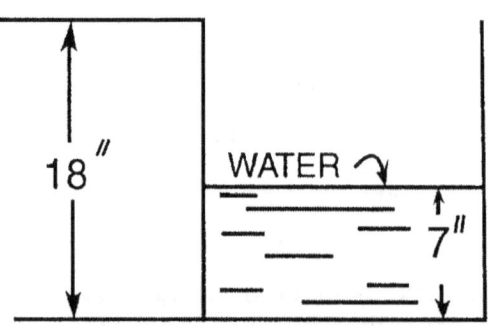

The percentage of the above tank that is filled with water is MOST NEARLY

   A. 33   B. 35   C. 37   D. 39

44.

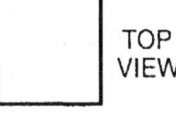 TOP VIEW

 FRONT VIEW

The top and front view of an object are shown above. The right side view will MOST likely look like

A. 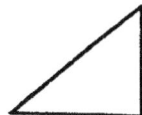   B. 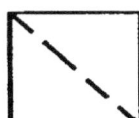   C.    D.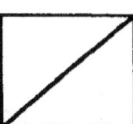

45.

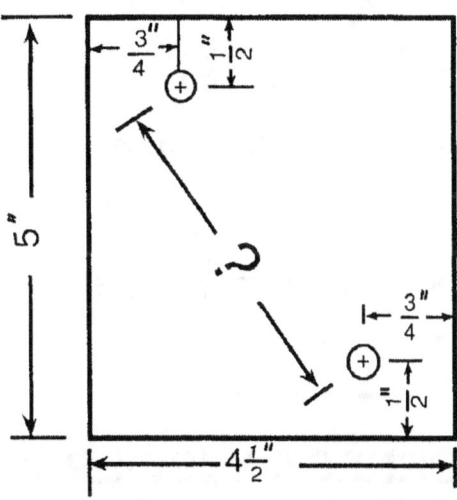

The distance between centers of the holes in the above diagram is MOST NEARLY

A. $4\frac{1}{2}"$ B. 4 3/4"   C. 5"   D. $5\frac{1}{4}"$

Questions 46-48.

DIRECTIONS: Questions 46 through 48, inclusive, are to be answered in accordance with the paragraph below.

A steam heating system with steam having a pressure of less than 10 pounds is called a low-pressure system. The majority of steam-heating systems are of this type. The steam may be provided by low-pressure boilers installed expressly for the purpose, or it may be gener-

ated in boilers at a higher pressure and reduced in pressure before admitted to the heating mains. In other instances, it may be possible to use exhaust steam which has been made to run engines and other machines and which still contains enough heat to be utilized in the heating system. The first case represents the system of heating used in the ordinary residence or other small building; the other two represent the systems of heating employed in industrial buildings where a power plant is installed for general power purposes.

46. According to the above paragraph, whether or not a steam heating system is considered a low pressure system is determined by the pressure

    A. generated by the boiler
    B. in the heating main
    C. at the inlet side of the reducing valve
    D. of the exhaust

46.____

47. According to the above paragraph, steam used for heating is sometimes obtained from steam

    A. generated principally to operate machinery
    B. exhausted from larger boilers
    C. generated at low pressure and brought up to high pressure before being used
    D. generated by engines other than boilers

47.____

48. As used in the above paragraph, the word *expressly* means

    A. rapidly
    C. usually
    B. specifically
    D. mainly

48.____

49. Of the following words, the one that is CORRECTLY spelled is

    A. suficient
    C. sufficient
    B. sufficiant
    D. suficiant

49.____

50. Of the following words, the one that is CORRECTLY spelled is

    A. fairly   B. fairley   C. farely   D. fairlie

50.____

KEY (CORRECT ANSWERS)

1. B	11. B	21. C	31. B	41. D
2. A	12. D	22. C	32. A	42. B
3. A	13. D	23. B	33. D	43. D
4. C	14. B	24. A	34. B	44. A
5. C	15. C	25. C	35. D	45. C
6. C	16. C	26. C	36. A	46. B
7. B	17. B	27. B	37. B	47. A
8. A	18. D	28. B	38. B	48. B
9. C	19. B	29. A	39. C	49. C
10. B	20. A	30. B	40. D	50. A

ARITHMETICAL REASONING
EXAMINATION SECTION
TEST 1

DIRECTIONS: Each question or incomplete statement is followed by several suggested answers or completions. Select the one that BEST answers the question or completes the statement. *PRINT THE LETTER OF THE CORRECT ANSWER IN THE SPACE AT THE RIGHT.*

1. Assume that a room measures 12'6" x 11'4". Its area is MOST NEARLY _____ sq. ft. 1._____
   A. 138 B. 139
   C. 140 D. 142

2. The SMALLEST subdivision found on the ordinary six-foot wooden rule is 2._____
   A. 1/32"   B. 1/16"   C. 1/8"   D. 1/4"

3. The sum of the following numbers, 6 1/4, 5 3/16, 7 1/2, 8 1/8, and 7 5/16, is 3._____
   A. 34 1/4   B. 34 5/16   C. 34 3/8   D. 34 7/16

4. 92796 divided by 376 is MOST NEARLY 4._____
   A. 245   B. 247   C. 249   D. 251

5. Assume that an inspector will average 8 inspections per day. The number of days it will take seven inspectors to complete a total of 1,344 inspections at the same average rate is 5._____
   A. 24   B. 26   C. 28   D. 30

6. The MAXIMUM number of 3" x 5" pieces that can be cut from one sheet of 17" x 22" paper is 6._____
   A. 20   B. 21   C. 22   D. 23

7. Suppose you are told to print a year's supply of a form. If 1,500 copies are used each month and the form is printed three up on an 8 1/2" x 14" sheet and cut to 4 1/2" x 8 1/2", how many 8 1/2" x 14" sheets are needed (disregarding waste)? 7._____
   A. 3,000   B. 4,500   C. 5,400   D. 6,000

8. The MAXIMUM number of 4" x 5" pieces that can be cut from five 500-sheet packages of 16" x 21" paper is 8._____
   A. 30,000   B. 40,000   C. 50,000   D. 60,000

9. The manager of the project has asked you to compute the cost of 175 feet of electric wire needed for an installation in the project community room. This wire is listed in the catalog in 1,000-foot coils, each coil weighing 32 pounds and costing $1.14 a pound.
The cost of the wire to be used is MOST NEARLY 9._____
   A. $4.35   B. $5.94   C. $6.24   D. $6.39

10. One section of a project containing 800 apartments was constructed at a cost of $116,000 per apartment. The two remaining sections of the project, containing 625 apartments each, are still to be built.
    In order that the average construction cost per apartment for the entire project will not exceed $130,000, the cost per apartment in the two sections still to be built should be APPROXIMATELY

    A. $131,000   B. $135,000   C. $139,000   D. $140,000

11. A certain project contains 57 two-room apartments (for 2 persons), 305 three-room apartments (for 3 persons), 309 four-room apartments (for 4 persons), 104 five-room apartments (for 4 persons), 197 five-room apartments (for 5 persons), and 52 five-room apartments (for 6 persons).
    The percentage of 4-person apartments in this project is between

    A. 10 and 19.9   B. 20 and 29.9
    C. 30 and 39.9   D. 40 and 49.9

12. Assume that each year the value of a certain project depreciates 2 1/2% of its original value.
    At the end of the third year, its value, after depreciation, is $6,734,900. The original value was MOST NEARLY

    A. $7,252,000   B. $7,253,000
    C. $7,280,000   D. $7,290,000

13. A housing project with A apartments contains a total of R rooms. The total number of residents is N.
    The number of residents per apartment is expressed by

    A. N/A   B. R/A   C. A/N   D. N/R

14. A unit of ten housing assistants has been assigned the job of interviewing 1,800 applicants. They are each able to do two interviews an hour. After the job is one-third done, an improvement in the procedure is put into effect which makes it possible to save 25% of the time.
    The number of 7-hour days required for the entire job is MOST NEARLY

    A. 10   B. 11   C. 12   D. 13

15. Assume that 135,200 new applications were received in a certain year for the 9,500 apartments made available in new projects. In addition, 32,900 old applications were reviewed for eligibility for the new apartments. Of these, 49,300 new and 9,400 old applicants were found eligible.
    The percentage of eligible applicants who will NOT receive an apartment is

    A. under 75%   B. between 75% and 80%
    C. between 80% and 85%   D. over 85%

16. A project tenant who is a cabdriver works on a commission basis, receiving 42 1/2% *of* the fares. In addition, his earnings from tips are valued at 29% of the commissions. If his average monthly fares equal $520, then his annual earnings are

    A. between $3,000 and $3,400   B. between $3,400 and $3,800
    C. between $3,800 and $4,200   D. over $4,200

17. A project tenant's earning record for the year is as follows: up to January 15, unemployed; continuously employed for the rest of the year; from Monday, January 16, $430 a week; from Monday, April 3, $390 a week; from Monday, October 2, $450 a week. This tenant's yearly income is MOST NEARLY

   A. $15,000   B. $17,500   C. $21,000   D. $22,500

17.____

18. In a certain city in 2000, the average cost for constructing one apartment of a public housing project was $127,500, an increase of 4% over 1999.
   The cost of constructing a project of 1,500 apartments in 2000 was more than in 1999 by an amount which is MOST NEARLY

   A. $6,000,000   B. $6,150,000
   C. $7,400,000   D. $7,650,000

18.____

Questions 19-20.

DIRECTIONS: Questions 19 and 20 are to be answered SOLELY on the basis of the following paragraph.

A housing development has 450 apartments. The average weekly rent is $134.50 per apartment. The average amount of subsidy money added to the average weekly rent (to meet the total operating costs) is $68.00. Since the time when the amount of the subsidy was determined, operating costs for the development have increased by $3,960.00 per week.

19. If the subsidy is increased by 6%, what INCREASE in the average weekly rental will be necessary to meet monthly operating costs?

   A. $3.40   B. $4.72
   C. $8.80   D. No increase

19.____

20. What is the NEW total weekly operating cost per apartment?

   A. $76.80   B. $143.30   C. $211.30   D. $242.10

20.____

21. In a certain housing project, the average income of tenant families is $19,400 per annum and the average rent per apartment is $360 per month.
   If the average income increases 12% in a year while the average rent of an apartment increases 15%, how much MORE money will the average family have in a year after paying rent?

   A. $677.60   B. $1,680.00   C. $2,241.60   D. $4,968.00

21.____

22. A certain housing project has 1,860 tenant families. It has two playgrounds, both rectangular in shape. One measures 104 feet by 45 feet; the other is 74 feet by 53 feet.
   The number of square feet of playground space per family in this project is MOST NEARLY

   A. 3   B. 5   C. 7   D. 9

22.____

4 (#1)

23. A particular housing project has 1,460 occupied apartments. If there are 12 new tenants in January, 14 in February, and 16 in March, the turnover rate for the first quarter of the year is MOST NEARLY   23.____

   A. 2.9%   B. 3.2%   C. 3.5%   D. 3.8%

24. In 2009, the cost of refrigerator repairs and maintenance at a certain housing project was $2,700 more than in 2008, representing an increase of 18%. A further increase at the same rate is expected in 2010.
   The cost of refrigerator repairs and maintenance in 2010 will be MOST NEARLY   24.____

   A. $6,000   B. $10,000   C. $18,000   D. $21,000

25. If a tenant earns $31,680 a year and his rent is 25% of his annual income, the amount of rent he pays each month is   25.____

   A. $660   B. $690   C. $720   D. $810

KEY (CORRECT ANSWERS)

1. D		11. D	
2. B		12. C	
3. C		13. A	
4. B		14. B	
5. A		15. C	
6. B		16. B	
7. D		17. C	
8. B		18. C	
9. D		19. B	
10. C		20. C	

21. B
22. B
23. A
24. D
25. A

SOLUTIONS TO PROBLEMS

1. Area = (12.5')(11 1/3') = 141 2/3 sq.ft. ≈ 142 sq.ft.

2. 1/16" the smallest marking on a six-foot wooden ruler.

3. 6 1/4 + 5 3/16 + 7 1/2 + 8 1/8 + 7 5/16 = 33 22/16 = 34 3/8

4. 92,796 ÷ 376 ≈ 246.8 ≈ 247

5. 7 inspectors can do a total of 56 inspections per day. Then, 1344 ÷ 56 = 24 days

6.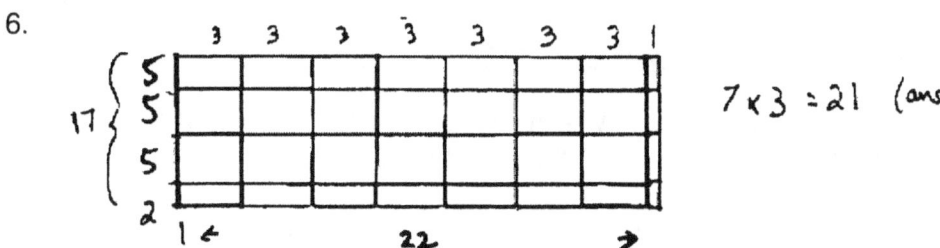

7. Each year, (1500)(12) = 18,000 forms are needed. Since 3 forms can fit on each sheet, 18,000 ÷ 3 = 6000 sheets are needed.

8. 16" ÷ 4" = 4 and 21" ÷ 5" rounds down to 4. Then, (4)(4) = 16 pieces of dimensions 4"x5" can be cut from each original 16"x21" piece of paper. For 2500 original sheets, we can cut (2500)(16) = 40,000 4"x5" pieces.

9. Let x = weight of the 175-ft. wire. x/175 = 32/1000. Solving, x = 5.6 lbs. The cost of this wire = (5.6)($1.14) = $6.38

10. Let x = cost per apartment for the remaining 1250 apartments. Then, [(800)($116,000)+1250x]/2050 < $130,000. Simplifying, $92,800,000 + 1250x < $266,500,000. Solving, x < $138,960 or approx. $139,000.

11. (309+104) ÷ (57+305+309+104+197+52) = 413/1024 = 40.33%

12. .925x = 6,734,900; x = 7,280,000

13. If A apartments contain N residents, the number of residents per apartment = N/A

14. (10)(2) = 20 applicants can be interviewed in 1 hour. Then, 600 ÷ 20 = 30 hours. The remaining 1200 applicants would normally require an additional 1200 ÷ 20 = 60 hours; however, the new procedure of interviewing these 1200 applicants will take (60)(.75) = 45 hours. Total time for all 1800 applicants = 30 + 45 = 75 hours. Finally, 75 ÷ 7 = 10.7 ≈ 11 days. (using 7 hours = 1 day)

15. 49,300 + 9,400 = 58,700 eligible applicants. Since only 9500 apartments are available, 49,200 eligible applicants will not receive an apartment. Finally, 49,200 ÷ 58,700 = 83.8%.

16. If his monthly fare averages $520, he gets a commission of ($520)(.425) = $221 and tips of ($221)(.29) ~ $64. His annual earnings = (12)($221+$64) = $3420.

17. (11)($430) + (26)($390) + (13)($450) = $20,720 = $21,000

18. The cost for one apartment in 1999 was $127,500 * 1,04 = $122,596. The cost difference per apartment from 1999 to 2000 was ~ $4904. For 1500 apartments, the additional cost was (1500)($4904) = $7,356,000 ~ $7,400,000.

19. $3960 ÷ 450 = $8.80 required increase per apartment to meet new operating costs. The increase in the subsidy = (.06)($68) = $4.08. The weekly rental increase necessary = $8.80 - $4.08 = $4.72

20. New operating cost per apartment (weekly) = $134.50 + $68 + $8.80 = $211.30

21. $19,400 - (12)($360) = $15,080. The new annual income = ($19,400)(1.12) = $21,728 and the new monthly rent = ($360X1.15) = $414. Then, $21,728 - (12)($414) = $16,760. Finally, $16,760 - $15,080 = $1680

22. (104)(45) + (74)(53) = 8602 sq.ft. Then, 8602 ÷ 1860 ≈ 5

23. (12+14+16) ÷ 1460 = 42/1460 ≈ 2.9%

24. The cost in 2008 was $2700 ÷ .18 = $15,000. Thus, the cost in 2009 was $15,000 + 2700 = $17,700. Finally, the cost in 2010 was ($17,700X1.18) = $20,886 = $21,000

25. (.25)($31,680) = $7,920. Then, $7,920   12 = $660

TEST 2

DIRECTIONS: Each question or incomplete statement is followed by several suggested answers or completions. Select the one that BEST answers the question or completes the statement. *PRINT THE LETTER OF THE CORRECT ANSWER IN THE SPACE AT THE RIGHT.*

1. The area of the plot plan shown at the right is _____ square feet.
   A. 25,300
   B. 26,700
   C. 28,100
   D. 30,500

   1._____

2. A pump that removes 30 gallons of water per minute is pumping water from a cellar 30 feet x 50 feet covered with eight inches of water. One cubic foot of water equals 7.5 gallons of water.
   The number of minutes it will take to remove the eight inches of water from the cellar is

   A. 200   B. 225   C. 250   D. 275

   2._____

3. In order to clean an office with 20,000 sq.ft. of space in 4 hours using a standard of 900 sq.ft. per hour, the number of cleaners you should assign to do the job is MOST NEARLY

   A. 4   B. 6   C. 8   D. 10

   3._____

4. The area of a floor 35' wide and 45' long is, in square yards, MOST NEARLY

   A. 175   B. 262   C. 525   D. 1,575

   4._____

Questions 5-6.

DIRECTIONS: Questions 5 and 6 are to be answered on the basis of the following paragraph.

A tenant in a housing development receives a semi-monthly public assistance check of $468 and pays a monthly rental of $284 from the proceeds. The tenant is about to begin paying $36 additional per month toward total rent arrears of $544. At the same time that the arrears payments begin, his semi-monthly check increases to $484.

5. What will be the TOTAL change in monthly net income after all rent payments?

   A. $12   B. $8   C. $4   D. No change

   5._____

6. If, instead of paying only $36 per month toward the arrears, the total increase in public assistance payments is used to increase arrears payments, how many months will it take the tenant to pay off the arrears? _____ months.

   A. 8   B. 10   C. 12   D. 14

   6._____

7. A tenant is offered two options in renewing a lease:
   (1) a one-year lease at a 10% increase in rent, or
   (2) a three-year lease at an 18% increase in rent.
   The tenant's current rent is $220 monthly.
   If the tenant takes the first option and continues to live in the apartment for three years with a 10% increase in rent each year, what would be the DIFFERENCE between the total rent he would pay and the rent he would have paid had he chosen the three-year lease?

   A. $266.64   B. $276.64   C. $1,425.60   D. $1,692.24

8. A certain task that an assistant performs takes approximately 45 minutes per unit of work. Seventy-five percent of his work day is spent on this task.
   Assuming that he works seven hours per day, how many work days will it take him to finish 1,470 units of work?

   A. 153   B. 210   C. 240   D. 270

9. It takes 5 1/2 gallons of paint to paint an average apartment, and it requires 18 man hours.
   If the price of paint increases $2.40 per gallon and the pay of the painters increases $2.65 per hour, what is the INCREASE in the cost of painting an apartment?

   A. $49.90   B. $50.90   C. $59.90   D. $60.90

10. A government employee can process a certain type of report in 23 minutes.
    How many such reports could he finish processing in a work day from 9:00 A.M. to 5:00 P.M., with a 45-minute lunch break and two 10-minute coffee breaks?

    A. 16   B. 17   C. 18   D. 19

11. The income of a tenant family is as follows: The husband has a gross income of $280 per week; the wife has a gross income of $220 per week. Deductions from gross family income total $116 per week, plus an allowable child care expense of $56 per week.
    What is the net annual income of the family after deductions and allowable child care expenses?

    A. $16,656   B. $17,056   C. $18,656   D. $19,056

12. Assume that you receive the following bills and coins for use as a change fund: 180 twenty-dollar bills, 110 ten-dollar bills, 125 five-dollar bills, 100 one-dollar bills, 200 quarters, 125 dimes, 50 nickels, and 150 pennies. You cash checks for tenants out of this fund in the following amounts: $134.96, $83.84, $76.96, and $74.37.
    The BALANCE in the fund after paying out these amounts should be

    A. $4,096.37   B. $5,021.47   C. $5,121.37   D. $5,233.87

13. Suppose that a tenant has paid a rent of $312.80 per month for six months and the rent is then increased by 5%.
    After paying the increased rent for six months, how much MORE money has the tenant paid in rent than was paid in the previous six months?

    A. $15.64   B. $93.84   C. $112.56   D. $187.68

14. Assume that $13,965.31 was collected at a project on a Monday.
    If the collections at this project on Tuesday were 7% more than on Monday, then the Tuesday total was MOST NEARLY

    A. $12,987.74   B. $14,492.90
    C. $14,942.88   D. $14,977.57

15. Suppose that $12,864 was collected on a Thursday and $17,243 was collected on Friday.
    The percentage increase in Friday's collections over Thursday's collections was MOST NEARLY

    A. 25%   B. 34%   C. 66%   D. 75%

16. If the total monthly rent roll at Project Y is $116,610 and the cash collections of current rent at the end of the first week of the month totaled 93% of the total monthly rent roll, then the amount of current rent still uncollected was

    A. $7,160.70   B. $8,162.70
    C. $8,273.30   D. $8,621.30

17. A city employee whose weekly pay was $432.60 for a 35-hour work week was required to work 7 hours overtime during one week. The employee asked what the pay rate was for this overtime and was informed that the first five hours would be paid at his regular hourly rate and the next two hours at one and one-half times his regular rate.
    According to this information, the total amount of pay for overtime worked by this employee during this week was

    A. $61.80   B. $86.52   C. $98.88   D. $136.68

18. If 3/4 of a number is 10 more than 1/2 the number, the number is

    A. 8   B. 20   C. 40   D. 50

19. Instead of dividing a number by 5, you can achieve the same result by

    A. multiplying by 1/2   B. dividing by 1/2
    C. multiplying by .2   D. dividing by .2

20. What percent of 4/5 is 7/10?

    A. 56%   B. 87 1/2%   C. 114 2/7%   D. 178 4/7%

21. When a number is multiplied by three and then divided by 1/4, the net result is that the number is

    A. multiplied by 3/4   B. multiplied by 4/3
    C. multiplied by 12   D. divided by 12

22. Three tellers, all working at the same rate of speed, were able to post 1,260 rent charges in 14 hours.
    How long would the job have taken if only two of these tellers had been assigned?
    _____ hours.

    A. 7   B. 9 1/3   C. 18   D. 21

4 (#2)

23. A teller filed 440 ledger cards in an hour. If this amounted to 12 1/2% of the task, what was the TOTAL number of cards he was required to file? 23.____

    A. 360   B. 3,520   C. 3,600   D. 5,402

24. $5,470.80 is to be paid to 47 employees, each of whom will receive the same amount in cash. 24.____
If in making the payment you give each employee the minimum number of bills and coins possible, how many $1 bills will you need to meet the payroll?

    A. 47   B. 94   C. 188   D. 282

25. A commercial tenant pays an annual rental under a graduated percentage lease. The annual rental is based on gross sales for the year and is computed as follows: 25.____

    On the first $50,000 of gross sales   - 5%
    On the next $25,000   - 4 1/2%
    On the next $15,000   - 3 1/2%
    On the next $10,000   - 2 1/2%
    On sales in excess of $100,000   - 1 1/4%

His gross sales for the year were $116,292.80.
His rental for that year was MOST NEARLY

    A. $2,703.60   B. $4,603.60
    C. $5,203.60   D. $11,453.60

KEY (CORRECT ANSWERS)

1. C
2. C
3. B
4. A
5. C

6. A
7. A
8. B
9. D
10. C

11. B
12. C
13. B
14. C
15. B

16. B
17. C
18. C
19. C
20. B

21. C
22. D
23. B
24. A
25. B

SOLUTIONS TO PROBLEMS

1. Using a horizontal dotted line, we construct two rectangles. Total area = (270')(70') + (115')(150'-70') = 28,100 sq.ft.

2. (30')(50')(2/3') = 1000 cu.ft., which contains (1000)(7.5) = 7500 gallons. Then, 7500 ÷ 30 = 250 minutes

3. 20,000 ÷ 900 = 22.$\bar{2}$ man-hours. To complete the job in 4 hours, use 22.2 ÷ 4 ≈ 6 cleaners.

4. (35')(45') = 1575 sq.ft. Then, 1575 ÷ 9 = 175 sq.yds.

5. ($468)(2) - $284 = $652 net income. With changes, ($484)(2) - $320 = $648 new net income. Monthly net income = $4

6. ($484)(2) - ($468)(2) = $32. Then, $32 + $36 = $68. Finally, $544 ┬ $68 = 8 months.

7.
Yr. 1: $242 x 12 =	2904.00
Yr. 2: + 10% + $290.40 =	3194.40
Yr. 3: + 10% + $310.44 =	3573.84
	9612.24

    9612.24 9612.24 - 9345.60 = $266.64

8. (.75)(7) = 5.25 hrs. assigned to this task per day. 1470 units of work will require (1470)(45) = 66,150 min. Since he has 5.25 hours = 315 min. each day, the number of days needed = 66,150 ÷ 315 = 210.

9. Change in cost = ($2.40)(5.5) + ($2.65)(18) = $60.90

10. From 9:00 AM to 5:00 PM is 8 hours. Then, 480 - 45 - (2)(10) = 415 min. Finally, 415 ÷ 23 = 18

11. $280 + $220 - $116 - $56 = $328. Then, ($328)(52) = $17,056 annually.

12. (180)($20) + (110)($10) + (125)($5) + (100)($1) + (200)($0.25) + (125)($0.10) + (50)($0.05) + (150)($0.01) - $134.96 - $83.84 - $76.96 - $74.37 = $5121.37

13. ($312.80)(6) = $1876.80. With the 5% increase, (312.80)(1.05)(6) = $1970.64. The additional cost = $93.84

14. ($13,965.31)(1.07) = $14,942.88

15. $17,243 - $12,864 = $4379. Then, $\frac{\$4379}{\$12,864} \approx 34\%$

16. Amount uncollected = (.07)($116,610) = $8162.70

17. $432.60 ÷ 35 = $12.36 per hour on regular pay. His overtime pay per hour = ($12.36)(1.5) = $18.54. His pay for extra time = (5)($12.36) + (2)($18.54) = $98.88.

18. Let x = missing number. Then, $3/4\, x = 10 + 1/2\, x$. Simplifying, $1/4\, x = 10$. Solving, $x = 40$

19. Dividing by 5 is equivalent to multiplying by $1/5 = .2$

20. $$\frac{7}{10} \div \frac{4}{5} = \frac{7}{10} \cdot \frac{5}{4} = \frac{7}{8} = 87.5\%$$

21. Since dividing by 1/4 means multiplying by 4, the net result for the given statement is multiplying by $(3)(4) = 12$

22. $(3)(14) = 42$ worker-hours. Then, $42 \div 2 = 21$ hours

23. $440 \div .125 = 3520$ ledger cards

24. $\$5470.80 \div 47 = \$116.40$. By using the minimum number of bills, each employee would receive one $1 bill toward the $116.40. Thus, for 47 employees, 47 $1 bills would be needed.

25. Total rental - $(.05)(\$50{,}000) + (.045)(\$25{,}000) + (.035)(\$15{,}000) + (.025)(\$10{,}000) + (.0125 \times 16{,}292.80) = \$4603.66 \approx \$4603.60$

TEST 3

DIRECTIONS: Each question or incomplete statement is followed by several suggested answers or completions. Select the one that BEST answers the question or completes the statement. *PRINT THE LETTER OF THE CORRECT ANSWER IN THE SPACE AT THE RIGHT.*

1. 1/6 is the same as

    A. .16 2/3% B. 16 2/3% C. .165 D. 16 2/3

2. 205% written as a decimal is

    A. .0205 B. .205 C. 2.05 D. 20.5

3. The sum of the fractions 2/3, 2/4, 5/6, and 7/8 is

    A. 1 15/16 B. 2 1/4 C. 2 3/4 D. 2 7/8

4. 24 3/8 multiplied by 48 amounts to

    A. 1,115 B. 1,121 C. 1,160 D. 1,170

5. One hundred pennies weigh 15 oz.
   The value of 4 lbs., 5 oz. of pennies is

    A. $4.33 B. $4.50 C. $4.60 D. $5.13

6. Which of the following is GREATER than .5?

    A. 1/8 B. 5/9 C. 5.5% D. 20%

7. A recreation leader and his assistant arranged a picnic in the country for a group of 20 project tenants. Five tenants went in the leader's car and five went in the assistant's car, each tenant paying his driver $1.30 for the roundtrip. The ten tenants who went by bus paid $2.50 for the roundtrip. It was agreed that the tenants who went by car would each pay an additional amount which would be distributed to the tenants who went by bus so that all the tenants would pay the same amount for transportation.
   What ADDITIONAL amount would a tenant who went by car pay?

    A. 60¢ B. 70¢ C. 90¢ D. $1.20

8. An employee whose normal work day was 7 hours was required to work overtime, for which he took compensatory time off on an hour-for-hour basis in lieu of overtime pay. In a month with 21 working days, he worked as follows:
   First week - worked overtime 5 1/2 hours and took off 4 1/4 hours
   Second week - worked overtime 10 hours and took off 10 1/2 hours
   Third week - took one vacation day
   Balance of month - worked regular schedule
   How many hours did he work during the month?

    A. 129 3/4 B. 135 1/4 C. 139 3/4 D. 140 3/4

9. Suppose that you have received the following bills and coins for use as a change fund: 230 twenty-dollar bills, 130 ten-dollar bills, 175 five-dollar bills, 150 one-dollar bills, 220 quarters, 150 dimes, 60 nickels, and 200 pennies. You cash checks for tenants out of this fund in the following amounts: $120.75, $95.57, $75.40, and $48.50.
The balance of cash in the fund after paying out these amounts SHOULD be

   A. $5,159.88   B. $5,659.78   C. $6,649.88   D. $6,659.78

10. A caretaker received $350 for having worked from Monday through Friday, 9 A.M. to 5 P.M. with one hour a day for lunch.
The number of hours the caretaker would have to work to earn $60 is

   A. 10   B. 6
   C. 70 divided by 12   D. 70 minus 12

11. If the cost of a broom went up from $8.00 to $12.00, the percent INCREASE in the original cost is

   A. A. 20   B. 25   C. 33 1/3   D. 50

12. The AVERAGE of the numbers 3, 5, 7, 8, 12 is

   A. 5   B. 6   C. 7   D. 8

13. The cost of 100 bags of cotton cleaning cloths, 89 pounds per bag, at 70 cents per pound, is

   A. $5,493.50   B. $6,230.00   C. $7,000.00   D. $8,900.00

14. If 5 1/2 bags of sweeping compound cost $55.00, then 6 1/2 bags would cost

   A. $60.00   B. $62.50   C. $65.00   D. $67.50

15. The cost of cleaning supplies in a project averaged $3,300 a month during the first 8 months of the year.
How much can be spent each month for the last four months if the total amount that can be spent for cleaning supplies for the year is $38,800?

   A. $1,240   B. $2,200   C. $3,100   D. $3,300

16. A shelf in a supply closet can safely hold only 100 pounds. A package of paper towels weighs 2 pounds, a carton of disinfectant weighs 8 pounds, and a box of soap weighs 1 pound. There are already 6 cartons of disinfectant and 6 boxes of soap on the shelf.
How many packages of towels can be SAFELY placed there?

   A. 20   B. 23   C. 25   D. 27

17. A cleaning solution is made up of 4 gallons of water, 1 pint of liquid soap, and 1 pint of ammonia.
How many gallons of water are needed to use up a gallon of ammonia?
_____ gallons.

   A. 8   B. 16   C. 24   D. 32

18. Suppose a caretaker has 50 stair halls to clean.
If he cleans 74% of them, the number of stair halls still UNCLEANED is

   A. 38   B. 26   C. 24   D. 13

19. If a man has a 12-foot piece of wood and wishes to cut it into two pieces so that one piece is twice as long as the other, the LONGER piece should be _____ feet.

    A. 7   B. 7 1/2   C. 8   D. 8 1/2

20. A city employee, whose weekly salary is $537.60 for a 35-hour workweek, was required to work 7 hours overtime during one week. The employee asked what the pay rate was for this overtime and was informed that he would be paid for the first five hours at his regular hourly rate and the next two hours at one and one-half times his regular hourly rate. According to this information, the GROSS pay for overtime worked by this employee during this week was

    A. $76.80   B. $107.52   C. $122.88   D. $161.28

21. Assume that you receive the following bills and coins for use as a change fund: 120 twenty-dollar bills, 150 ten-dollar bills, 100 five-dollar bills, 100 one-dollar bills, 100 quarters, 50 dimes, 25 nickels, and 200 pennies. You cash checks for tenants out of this fund in the following amounts: $189.30, $87.16, $72.90, and $68.50.
    The cash balance in the fund after cashing these checks should be

    A. $4,115.39   B. $4,325.01
    C. $4,713.09   D. $4,951.11

22. If the total monthly rent roll at Project X is $121,990 and the cash collections of current rent at the end of the first week of the month were 95% of the total monthly rent roll, then the amount of current rent still uncollected was

    A. $5,679.90   B. $6,099.50
    C. $6,211.90   D. $6,312.50

23. Suppose that a tenant has paid $172.40 per month in rent for six months and the rent is then increased by 5%. After paying the increased rent for six months, how much MORE money has the tenant paid in rent than was paid in the previous six months?

    A. $8.62   B. $51.72   C. $57.52   D. $60.58

24. The rents for three families in a relocation site come to a total of $9,720 per year.
    If Family A pays $3,480 per year and Family B pays $2,400 per year, how much does Family C pay?

    A. $2,760   B. $3,840   C. $4,200   D. $5,800

25. In a certain project, an exterminator is told to spray 120 apartments, 40 apartments, 20 basements, 80 apartments, 50 storerooms, and 10 compactors.
    The TOTAL number of apartments which should be sprayed is

    A. 240   B. 260   C. 310   D. 320

KEY (CORRECT ANSWERS)

1.	B	11.	D
2.	C	12.	C
3.	D	13.	B
4.	D	14.	C
5.	C	15.	C
6.	B	16.	B
7.	A	17.	D
8.	D	18.	D
9.	D	19.	C
10.	B	20.	C

21. A
22. B
23. B
24. B
25. A

SOLUTIONS TO PROBLEMS

1. $\frac{1}{6} = .\overline{16} = 16\frac{2}{3}\%$

2. 205% = 2.05

3. 2/3 + 2/4 + 5/6 + 7/8 = 69/24 = 2 7/8

4. (24 3/8)(48) = (24.375)(48) = 1170

5. 4 lbs. 5 oz. = 69 oz. Let x = required weight. Then, $\frac{\$1.00}{15} = \frac{x}{69}$ Solving, x = $4.60

6. $\frac{5}{9} = .\overline{5} > .5$

7. The total paid by all 20 tenants was (10)($1.30) + (10)($2.50) = $38.00. If each person had paid the same amount, it would be $38.00 v 20 = $1.90. So, the additional amount owed by each tenant who went by car was $0.60.

8. 1st week: 35 + 5 1/2 - 4 1/4 = 36 1/4 hrs. 2nd week: 35 + 10 - 10 1/2 = 34 1/2 hrs. 3rd week: (7) (4) = 28 hrs. Balance of month: (7)(21-15) = 42 hrs. Total hrs. = 140 3/4

9. (230)($20) + (130)($10) + (175)($5) + (150)($1) + (220)(.25) + (150)(.10) + (60)(.05) + (200)(.01) - $120.75 - $95.57 - $75.40 - $48.50 = $6659.78

10. 9 AM to 5 PM minus 1 hour for lunch = 35 hrs./wk. x = required number of hrs. Then, $\frac{\$350}{35} = \frac{\$60}{x}$. Solving, x = 6

11. ($12.00-$8.00) ÷ $8.00 = 4 = 50%

12. (3+5+7+8+12) ÷ 5 = 35 ÷ 5 = 7

13. (89)(100) = 8900 lbs. Then, (8900)($0.70) = $6230.00

14. Let x = cost. $\frac{5.5}{\$55} = \frac{6.5}{x}$. Solving, x = $65.00

15. $38,800 - (8)($3300) = $12,400. Then, $12,400 ÷ 4 = $3100

16. (6)(8) + (6)(1) = 54 lbs. Only 100 - 54 = 46 more pounds can be placed on the shelf. Finally, 46 ÷ 2 = 23 pkgs. of towels.

17. Since 8 pints = 1 gallon, a gallon of ammonia requires (8)(4) = 32 gallons of water.

18. (50)(.26) = 13 halls uncleaned

19. Let x = longer piece and 1/2 x = shorter piece. Then, x + 1/2 x = 12 So, 3/2 x = 12, and x = 8 feet

20. $537.60 ÷ 35 = $15.36 per hour for regular pay. Overtime pay per hour = (15.36)(1.5) = $23.04. His overtime pay = (5)($15.36) + (2)($23.04) = $122.88

21. (120)($20) + (150)($10) + (100)($5) + (100)($1) + (100)($0.25) + (50)($0.10) + (25)($0.05) + (200)($0.01) - $189.30 - $87.16 - $72.90 - $68.50 = $4115.39.

22. ($121,990)(.05) = $6099.50 uncollected

23. ($172.40)(1.05) = 181.02. Then, ($181.02)(6) - ($172.40)(6) = $51.72

24. Family C pays $9720 - $3480 - $2400 = $3840

25. 120 + 40 + 80 = 240 apartments

THE USE AND CARE OF TOOLS

CONTENTS

I. INTRODUCTION.
    1. Definitions
    2. Safety Precautions.

II. MEASURING TOOLS
    1. General
    2. Standards of Measurement
        a. Standards of Length
        b. Standards of Screw Threads
        c. Standards of Wire and Sheet Metal
        d. Standards of Weight
    3. Useful Measuring Tools
        a. Levels
        b. Plumb Bobs
        c. Scrivers
        d. Rules or Scales
        e. Precision Tapes
        f. Squares
        g. Calipers and Dividers h. Micrometers
        i. Surface, Depth, and Height Gages
        j. Plug, Ring, and Snap Gages and Gage Blocks
        k. Miscellaneous Measuring Gages

III. NONEDGED TOOLS
    1. General
    2. Useful Nonedged Tools
        a. Hammers and Mallets
        b. Screwdrivers
        c. Wrenches
        d. Pliers and Tongs
        e. Clamping Devices
        f. Jacks
        g. Bars and Mattock
        h. Soldering Irons
        i. Grinders and Sharpening Stones
        j. Benders and Pulters
        k. Torchers
        l. Blacksmith's Anvils and Iron Working Tools
        m. Breast Drill and Ratchet Bit Brace
        n. Sheet Metal Tools

IV. EDGED HANDTOOLS
    1. General
    2. Useful Edged Handtools
        a. Chisels
        b. Files
        c. Knives

d. Scrapers
e. Punches
f. Awls
g. Shears, Nippers, and Pincers h. Bolt, Cable, and Glass Cutters
i. Pipe and Tube Cutters, and Flaring Tools
j. Reamers
k. Taps and Dies
l. Thread Chasers
m. Screw and Tap Extractors

THE USE AND CARE OF TOOLS

I. INTRODUCTION

1. Definitions

    a. Handtools are defined as hand powered and hand operated tools that are designed to perform mechanical operations.
    b. Measuring tools are defined as tools that will measure work. Measuring tools can be classed as precision and non-precision tools.

2. Safety Precautions

    It is extremely important for all concerned to recognize the possibilities of injury when using handtools and measuring tools.
    The following safety precautions are included as a guide to prevent or minimize personal injury:

    a. Make certain all tool handles are securely attached before using them.
    b. Exercise extreme caution when handling edged tools.
    c. Do not use a tool for a purpose other than that for which it was intended.
    d. Do not handle tools carelessly carelessly piling tools in drawers, dropping tools on hard surfaces, etc., can damage tools. Damaged tools can cause mishaps.
    e. Keep your mind on your work so that you do not strike yourself or someone else with a hammer or sledge.
    f. Do not carry edged or pointed tools in your pocket.
    g. Always wear goggles when chipping metal and when grinding edges on tools.
    h. Hold driving tools correctly so that they will not slip off the work surface.
    i. Use the right tool for the job. The wrong tool may damage materials, injure workers, or both,
    j. Do not use punches with improper points or mushroomed heads,
    k. Do not use a tool that is oily or greasy. It may slip out of your hand, causing injury.
    l. When using jacks, make certain to use blocking or other supports when lifting a vehicle, in case of jack failure.
    m. Make sure work to be cut, sheared, chiseled, filed, etc., is steadied and secure, to prevent the tool from slipping.
    n. When using a knife, always cut away from your body, except in the case of a spoke shave or draw knife.
    o. Use torches and soldering irons with extreme care to prevent burns and explosions. The soldering iron must be so placed that the hot point cannot come in contact with flammable material or with the body.
    p. Familiarize yourself with the composition and hardness of the material to be worked.

II. MEASURING TOOLS

1. General

Measuring tools are designed for measuring work accurately. They include level indicating devices (levels), noncalibrated measuring tools (calipers, dividers, trammels) for transferring dimensions and/or layouts from one medium to another, calibrated measuring tools (rules, precision tapes, micrometers) designed to measure distances in accordance with one of several standards of measurement, gages (go and no-go gages, thread gages) which are machined to pre-determined shapes and/or sizes for measurement by comparison, and combination tools such as a combination square which is designed to perform two or more types of operation.

2. Standards of Measurement

a. Standards of Length

Two systems, the English and Metric, are commonly used in the design of measuring tools for linear measurements. The English system uses inches, feet, and yards, while the Metric system uses millimeters, centimeters, and meters. In relation to each other, 1 inch is equivalent to 25.4 millimeters, or 1 millimeter is equivalent to 0.039370 inch.

b. Standards of Screw Threads

There are several screw thread systems that are recognized as standards throughout the world. All threaded items for Ordnance use in the United States, Great Britain, and Canada are specified in the Unified System. The existing inch-measure screw-thread systems should be understood despite the existence of the Unified System.

(1) Inch-measure systems

(a) Whitworth

Introduced in England in 1941. The thread form is based on a 55 thread angle, and the crests and roots are rounded.

(b) American National

The American National screw-thread system was developed in 1933. This system is based on the 60 thread angle and the flat crests and roots and is included in the following series:
1. Coarse thread sizes of 1 to 12 and 1/4 to 4".
2. The fine thread series in sizes 0 to 12 and 1/4 to 1 1/2".
3. The extra-fine thread series in sizes 0 to 12 and 1/2 to 2".
4. The 8-pitch series in sizes from 1 to 6".
5. The 12-pitch series from 1/2 to 6".
6. The 16-pitch series from 3/4 to 4".

(c) Classes of fit

The American National screw-thread system calls for four regular classes of fit.

Class 1. - Loose fit, with no possibility for interference between screw and tapped hole.

2. - Medium or free fit, but permitting slight interference in the worst combination of maximum screw and maximum nut.
3. - Close tolerances on mating parts may require this fit, applied to the highest grade of interchangeable work.
4. - A fine snug fit, where a screwdriver or wrench may be necessary for assembly.

NOTE: An additional Class 5, or jaw fit, is recognized for studs.

(2) Unified system

Since the whitworth and American National thread forms do not assemble because of the difference in thread angle, the 60 thread angle was adapted in 1949; however, the British may still use rounded crests and roots and their products will assemble with those made in United States plants. In the Unified system, class signifies tolerance, or tolerance and allowance. It is determined by the selected combination of classes for mating external and internal threads. New classes of tolerance are listed below: 3 for screws, 1A, 2A, and 3A; and 3 for nuts, IB, 2B, and 3B.

(a) Classes 1A and 1B, loose fit

A fit giving quick and easy assembly, even when threads are bruised or dirty. Applications: Ordnance and special uses.

(b) Classes 2A and 2B, medium fit

This fit permits wrenching with minimum galling and seizure. This medium fit is suited for the majority of commercial fasteners and is interchangeable with the American National Class 2 fit.

(c) Classes 3A and 3B, close fit

No allowance is provided. Applications are those where close fit and accuracy of lead and thread angle are required.

c. Standards of Wire and Sheet Metal

Sheet metal, strip, wire, and tubing are produced with thickness diameters or wall thicknesses, according to several gaging systems, depending on the article and metal. This situation is the result of natural development and preferences of the industries that produce these products. No single standard for all manufacturers has been established, since practical considerations stand in the way of adoption. In the case of steel, large users are thoroughly familiar with the behavior of existing gages in tooling, especially dies, and do not intend that their shop personnel be burdened with learning how preferred thicknesses behave. Another important factor is the sum total of orders of warehouse stock manufactured with existing gages. You must keep abreast of any change in availability of metals in these common gaging systems, as opposed to simplified systems.

For example; in the brass industry, the American Standards Association (ASA) numbers are said to be preferred for simplicity of stocking, but actually most of the metal is still made to Brown and Sharpe (B&S) gage numbers.

(1) Sheet metal gaging systems

Several gaging systems are used for sheet and strip metal.

    (a)   Manufacturer's standard gaging system (Mfr's std)

This gaging system is currently used for carbon and alloy sheets. This system is based on steel weighing 41.82 psf, 1 inch thick. Gage thickness equivalents are based on 0.0014945 in. per oz. per sq. ft.; 0.023912 in. per lb. per sq. ft. (reciprocal of 41.82 lb. per sq. ft. per in. thick); 3.443329 in. per lb. per sq. in.

    (b) U.S. standard gaging system (U.S. std)

This gaging system is obsolete except for stainless steel sheets, cold-rolled steel strip (both carbon and alloy), stainless steel tubing, and nickel-alloy sheet and strip.

    (c) Birmingham wire gaging system (BWG)

This gaging system is also called the Stubs iron wire gaging system, and is used for hot-rolled steel carbon and alloy strip and steel tubing.

    (d) Brown and Sharpe, or American wire gaging system (B&S or AWG)

This gaging system is used for copper strip, brass and bronze sheet and strip, and aluminum and wire magnesium sheet.

(2) Wire gaging systems

    (a) Steel wire gaging system (SWG) or washburn & Moen gaging system

This gaging system is used for steel wire, carbon steel mechanical spring wire, alloy-steel spring wire, stainless steel wire, and so forth. Carbon steel or music wire (wire used in the manufacture of musical instruments) is nominally specified to the sizes in the American Steel & Wire Company music wire sizes, although it is referred to by a number of other names found in steel catalogs.

    (b) Brown & Sharpe (B&S) or American wire gaging system (AWG)

This gaging system is used for copper, copper alloy, aluminum, magnesium, nickel alloy, and other nonferrous metal wires used commercially.

(3) Rod gaging systems

The Brown & Sharpe gaging system is used for copper, brass, and aluminum rods. Steel rods are nominally listed in fractional sizes, but drill rod may be listed in stubs steel wire gage or the twist drill and steel wire gage. It is preferable to refer to twist drill sizes in inch equivalents instead of the Stubs or twist drill numbers.

d. Standards of Weight

Two standards of weight that are most commonly used are the Metric and English weight measures.

(1) Metric standards

The principal unit of weight in the Metric system is the gram (gm). Multiples of grams are obtained by prefixing the Greek words deka (10), hekto (100), and kilo (1,000). Divisions are obtained by prefixing the Latin words deci (1/10), centi (1/100), and milli (1/1000). The gram is the weight of 1 cubic centimeter of puje distilled water at a temperature of 39.2° F.; the kilogram is the weight of 1 liter (one cubic decimeter) of pureQdistilled water at a temperature of 39.2° F.; the metric ton is the weight of 1 cubic meter of pyre distilled water at a temperature of 39.2° F.

(2) English standards

The principal unit of weight in the English system is the grain (gr). We are more familiar with the ounce (oz), which is equal to 437.5 grains.

3. Useful Measuring Tools
   a. Levels
      (1) Purpose
         Levels are tools designed to prove whether a plane or surface is true horizontal or true vertical. Some levels are calibrated so that they will indicate the angle inclination in relation to a horizontal or vertical surface in degrees, minutes, and seconds.
   b. Plumb Bobs
      (1) Purpose
         The common plumb bob is used to determine true verticality. It is used in carpentry when erecting vertical uprights and corner posts of framework. Surveyors use it for transferring and lining up points. Special plumb bobs are designed for use with steel tapes or line to measure tank contents (oil, water, etc.).
   c. Scribers
      (1) Purpose
         Scribers are used to mark and lay out a pattern of work, to be followed in subsequent machining operations. Scribers are made for scribing, scoring, or marking many different materials such as glass, steel, aluminium, copper, and so forth.
   d. Rules or Scales
      (1) Purpose
         All rules (scales) are used to measure linear dimensions. They are read by a comparison of the etched lines on the scale with an edge or surface. Most scale dimensions are read with the naked eye, although a magnifying glass can be used to read graduations on a scale smaller than 1/64 inch.
   e. Precision Tapes
      (1) Purpose
         Precision tapes are used for measuring circumferences and long distances where rules cannot be applied.
   f. Squares
      (1) Purpose
         The purpose of a square is to test work for squareness and trueness. It is also used as a guide when marking work for subsequent machining, sawing, planing, and chiseling operations.
   g. Calipers and Dividers

6

    (1) Purpose

        Dividers are used for measuring distances between two points, for transferring or comparing measurements directly from a rule, or for scribing an arc, radius, or circle. Calipers are used for measuring diameters and distances, or for comparing dimensions or sizes with standards such as a graduated rule,

h. Micrometers

    (1) Purpose

        Micrometers are used for measurements requiring precise accuracy. They are more reliable and more accurate than the calipers listed in the preceding section.

i. Surface, Depth, and Height Gages

    (1) Purpose

        (a) Surface Gage

            A surface gage is a measuring tool generally used to transfer measurements to work by scribing a line, and to indicate the accuracy or parallelism of surfaces.

        (b) Depth Gage

            A depth gage is an instrument adapted to measuring the depth of holes, slots, counterborers, recesses, and the distance from a surface to some recessed part.

        (c) Height Gage

            A height gage is used in the layout of jigs and fixtures, and on a bench, where it is used to check the location of holes and surfaces. It accurately measures and marks off vertical distances from a plane surface.

        (d) Surface Plate

            A surface plate provides a true, smooth, plane surface. It is often used in conjunction with surface and height gages as a level base on which the gages and parts are placed to obtain accurate measurements,

j. Plug, Ring, and Snap Gages and Gage Blocks

    (1) Purpose

        Plug, ring, and snap gages, and precision gage blocks are used as standards to determine whether or not one or more dimensions of a manufactured part are within specified limits. Their measurements are included in the construction of each gage, and they are called fixed gages; however, some snap gages are adjustable. In the average shop, gages are used for a wide range of work, from rough machining to the finest tool and die making. The accuracy required of the same type gage will be different, depending on the application. The following classes of gages and their limits of accuracy are standard for all makes:

Class XX(Male gages only).
    Precision lapped to laboratory tolerances. For master or setup standards.

Class X

Precision lapped to close tolerances for many types of masters and the highest quality working and inspection gages.

Class Y

Good lapped finish to slightly increased tolerances for inspection and working gages.

Class Z

Commercial finish (ground and polished, but not fully lapped) for a large percentage of working gages in which tolerances are fairly wide, and where production quantities are not so large.

Class ZZ (Ring gages only)

Ground only to meet the demand for an inexpensive gage, where quantities are small and tolerances liberal.

k. Miscellaneous Measuring Gages
   (1) Purpose
    (a) Thickness (Feeler) Gages

     These gages are fixed in leaf form, which permits the checking and measuring of small openings such as contact points, narrow slots, and so forth. They are widely used to check the flatness of parts in straightening and grinding operations and in squaring objects with a try square.

    (b) Wire and Drill Gages

     The wire gage is used for gaging metal wire, and a similar gage is also used to check the size of hot and cold rolled steel, sheet and plate iron, and music wire. Drill gages determine the size of a drill and indicate the correct size of drill to use for given tap size. Drill number and decimal size are also shown in this type gage.

    (c) Drill Rods or Blanks

     Drill rods or blanks are used on line inspection work to check the size of drilled holes in the same manner as with plug gages. They are also used for setup inspection to check the location of holes.

    (d) Thread Gages

     Among the many gages used in connection with the machining and inspection of threads are the center gage and the screw pitch gages.

     1. Center gage

      The center gage is used to set thread cutting tools. Four scales on the gage are used for determining the number of threads per inch.

     2. Screw pitch gage

      Screw pitch gages are used to determine the pitch of an unknown thread. The pitch of a screw thread is the distance between the center of one tooth to the center of the next tooth.

    (e) Small Hole Gage Set

     This set of 4 or more gages is used to check dimensions of small holes, slots, groves etc., from approximately 1/8 to 1/2" in diameter.

(f) Telescoping Gages
These gages are used for measuring the inside size of slots or holes up to 6" in width or diameter.

(g) Thread Cutting Tool Gages
These gages provide a standard for thread cutting tools. They have an enclosed angle of 29 and include a 29 setting tool. One gage furnishes the correct form for square threads and the other for Acme standard threads.

(h) Fillet and Radius Gages
These gages are used to check convex and concave radii in corners or against shoulders.

(i) Drill Point Gage
This gage is used to check the accuracy of drill cutting edges after grinding. It is also equipped with a 6" hook rule. This tool can be used as a drill point gage, hook rule, plain rule, and a slide caliper for taking outside measurements.

(j) Marking Gages
A marking gage is used to mark off guidelines parallel to an edge, end, or surface of a piece of wood. It has a sharp spur or pin that does the marking.

(k) Tension Gage
This type of gage is used to check contact point pressure and brush spring tension in 1 ounce graduations.

(l) Saw Tooth Micrometer Gage
This special gage checks the depth of saw teeth in thousandths of an inch from 0 to 0.075 inch.

III. NONEDGED TOOLS
1. General

This title encompasses a large group of general purpose hand-tools. These tools are termed nonedged hand-tools because they are not used for cutting purposes and do not have sharpened or cutting edges. They are designed to facilitate mechanical operations such as clamping, hammering, twisting, turning, etc. This group includes such tools as hammers, mallets, and screwdrivers; which are commonly referred to as driving tools. Other types of nonedged tools are wrenches, pliers, clamps, pullers, soldering irons, torches, and many others of similar nature. Several types of pliers have cutting edges (exceptions to the rule).

2. Useful Nonedged Tools
   a. Hammers and Mallets
      (1) Purpose
         Hammers and mallets are used to drive nails, spikes, drift pins, bolts, and wedges. They are also used to strike chisels, punches, and to shape metals. Sledge hammers are used to drive spikes and large nails, to break rock and concrete, and to drift heavy timbers.
   b. Screwdrivers
      (1) Purpose

Screwdrivers are used for driving or removing screws or bolts with slotted or special heads.
- c. Wrenches
  - (1) Purpose

    Wrenches are used to tighten or loosen nuts, bolts, screws, and pipe plugs. Special wrenches are made to grip round stock, such as pipe, studs, and rods. Spanner wrenches are used to turn cover plates, rings and couplings.
- d. Pliers and Tongs
  - (1) Purpose

    Pliers are used for gripping, cutting, bending, forming, or holding work, and for special jobs. Tongs look like long-handled pliers and are mainly used for holding or handling hot pieces of metal work to be forged or quenched, or hot pieces of glass.
- e. Clamping Devices
  - (1) Purpose

    Vises are used for holding work on the bench when it is being planed, sawed, drilled, shaped, sharpened, riveted, or when wood is being glued. Clamps are used for holding work that cannot be satisfactorily held in a vise because of its shape or size, or when a vise is not available. Clamps are generally used for light work.
- f. Jacks
  - (1) Purpose

    Jacks are used to raise or lower work and heavy loads short distances. Some jacks are used for pushing and pulling operations, or for spreading and clamping.

- g. Bars and Mattock
  - (1) Purpose

    Bars are heavy steel tools used to lift and move heavy objects and to pry where leverage is needed. They are also used to remove nails and spikes during wrecking operations. The mattock is used for digging in hard ground, cutting Toots irnderground, und to loosen clay formations in which there is little or no rock. The mattock may also be used for light prying when no bars are available,
- h. Soldering Irons
  - (1) Purpose

    Soldering is joining two pieces of metal by adhesion. The soldering iron is the source of heat by melting solder and heating the parts to be joined to the proper temperature.
- i. Grinders and Sharpening Stones
  - (1) Purpose

    Grinders are devices that are designed to mount abrasive wheels that will wear away other materials to varying degrees. Special grinders are designed to receive engine valves. Sharpening stones are used for whetting or final sharpening of sharp edged tools that have been ground to shape or to a fine point on a grinder,
- j. Benders and Pullers
  - (1) Purpose

Benders are designed to facilitate bending brass or copper pipe and tubing. Pullers are designed to facilitate pulling operations such as removing bearings, gears, wheels, pulleys, sheaves, bushings, cylinder sleeves, shafts, and other close-fitting parts.

    k.   Torches

        (1)   Purpose

Torches are used as sources of heat in soldering, sweating, tinning, burning, and other miscellaneous jobs where heat is required.

    l.   Blacksmith's Anvils and Iron Working Tools

        (1)   Purpose

Blacksmith's anvils are designed to provide a working surface when punching holes through metal and for supporting the metal when it is being forged and shaped. Iron working tools such as flatters, fullers, swages, hardies, and set hammers are used to form or shape forgings. Heading tools are used to shape bolts.

    m.   Breast Drill and Ratchet Bit Brace

        (1)   Purpose

The breast drill and ratchet bit brace are used to hold various kinds of bits and twist drills used in boring and reaming holes and to drive screws, nuts, and bolts.

    n.   Sheet Metal Tools

        (1)   Purpose

Sheet metal working tools consist of stakes, dolly blocks, calking tools, rivet sets, and dolly bars. Punches, shears, and hammers are also sheet metal working tools. However, they are covered in other sections of this text. Rivet sets and dolly bars are used to form heads on rivets after joining sections of sheet metal and steel work. Stakes are used to support sheet metal while the metal is being shaped. Calking tools are used to shape joints of sheet metal. Dolly blocks are used conjunction with bumping body hammers to straighten out damaged sheet metal.

IV.   EDGED HANDTOOLS

    1.   General

Edged handtools are designed with sharp edges for working on metal, wood, plastic, leather, cloth, glass, and other materials. They are used to remove portions from the work or to separate the work into sections by cutting, punching, scraping, chiseling, filing, and so forth.

    2.   Useful Edged Eandtools

        a.   Chisels

          (1) Purpose

Chisels are made to cut wood, metal hard putty, and other materials. Woodworker's chisels are used to pare off and cut wood. Cold chisels are used to chip and cut cold metal. Some blacksmith's chisels are used to cut hot metal. A special chisel that is available is used to cut hard putty so that glass may be removed from its frame channel.

        b.   Files

          (1) Purpose

Files are used for cutting, smoothing off, or removing small amounts of metal.

c. Knives

(1) Purpose

Most knives are used to cut, pare, notch, and trim wood, leather, rubber, and other materials. Some knives used by glaziers are called putty knives; these are used to apply and spread putty when installing glass.

d. Scrapers

(1) Purpose

Some scrapers are used for trueing metal, wood, and plastic surfaces which have previously been machined or filed. Other scrapers are made to remove paint, stencil markings, and other coatings from various surfaces.

e. Punches

(1) Purpose

Punches are used to punch holes in metal, leather, paper, and other materials; mark metal, drive pins or rivets; to free frozen pins from their holes; and aline holes in different sections of metal. Special punches are designed to install grommets and snap fasteners. Bench mounted punching machines are used to punch holes in metal one at a time, or up to 12 holes simultaneously.

f. Awls

(1) Purpose

A saddler's awl is used for forcing holes in cloth or leather to make sewing easier. A scratch awl is used for making a center point or a small hole and for scribing lines on wood and plastics.

g. Shears, Nippers, and Pincers

(1) Purpose

Shears are used for cutting sheet metal and steel of various thicknesses and shapes. Nippers are used to cut metal off flush with a surface, and likewise to cut wire, light metal bars, bolts, and nails. Pincers are used to pull out nails, bolts, and pins.

h. Bolt, Cable, and Glass Cutters

(1) Purpose

Cutters or clippers are used to cut bolts, rods, wire rope, cable, screws, rivets, nuts, bars, strips, and wire. Special cutters are made to cut glass.

i. Piper and Tube Cutters, and Flaring Tools

(1) Purpose

Pipe cutters are used to cut pipe made of steel, brass, copper, wrought iron, and lead. Tube cutters are used to cut tube made of iron, steel, brass, copper, and aluminum. The essential difference is that tubing has considerably thinner walls are compared to pipe. Flaring tools are used to make single or double flares in the ends of tubing,

j. Reamers

(1) Purpose

Reamers are used to smoothly enlarge drilled holes to an exact size and to finish the hole at the same time. Reamers are also used to remove burrs from the inside diameters of pipe and drilled holes,

k. Taps and Dies
   (1) Purpose

Taps and dies are used to cut threads in metal, plastics, or hard rubber. The taps are used for cutting internal threads, and the dies are used to cut external threads.

l. Thread Chasers
   (1) Purpose

Thread chasers are used to re-thread damaged external or internal threads,

m. Screw and Tap Extractors
   (1) Purpose

Screw extractors are used to remove broken screws without damaging the surrounding material or the threaded hole. Tap extractors are used to remove broken taps.